STUDYING AT UN

How To Books for Students

Critical Thinking for Students
Getting a Job after University
Going to University
How to Know Your Rights: Students
How to Know Your Rights: Teachers
How to Master Book-Keeping
How to Master GCSE Accounts
How to Master Languages
How to Pass Exams Without Anxiety
How to Pass That Interview
How to Spend a Year Abroad
How to Start Word Processing
How to Study Abroad
How to Study & Learn

How to Study & Live in Britain
How to Survive at College
How to Use a Library
How to Write a Report
How to Write an Assignment
How to Write an Essay
How to Write Your Dissertation
Mastering Business English
Studying at University
Studying for a Degree
Taking in Students
Taking Your A-Levels
Writing Business Letters

Other titles in preparation

The How To series now contains more than 150 titles
in the following categories:

Business Basics
Family Reference
Jobs & Careers
Living & Working Abroad
Student Handbooks
Successful Writing

Please send for a free copy of the latest catalogue for full details
(see back cover for address).

STUDENT HANDBOOKS

STUDYING AT UNIVERSITY

How to make a success of
your academic course

Kevin Bucknall

How To Books

Cartoons by Mike Flanagan

British Library Cataloguing in Publication Data
A catalogue record for this book is available from the British Library.

First published in 1996 by How To Books Ltd, Plymbridge House, Estover
Road, Plymouth PL6 7PZ, United Kingdom. Tel: (01752) 202301.
Fax: (01752) 202331.

Note: The material contained in this book is set out in good faith for
general guidance and no liability can be accepted for loss or expense
incurred as a result of relying in particular circumstances on statements
made in the book. The laws and regulations are complex and liable to
change, and readers should check the current position with the relevant
authorities before making personal arrangements.

Produced for How To Books by Deer Park Productions.
Typeset by PDQ Typesetting, Stoke-on-Trent, Staffs.
Printed and bound by Cromwell Press, Broughton Gifford, Melksham,
Wiltshire.

Contents

List of Illustrations

Preface

Life is a wonderful journey through a fascinating world and going to university is a new and exciting stage, but it will involve changes on your part. This book will help you understand what goes on at university, tell you what you are expected to do, and explain how to do it. You will learn how to settle down and adapt quickly, learn more easily, get getter marks in assignments and develop marketable skills.

You can use the advice about learning in two possible ways: you can follow it in order to improve your marks and gain the best degree you possibly can; or you can follow it in order to minimise the amount of effort needed in order to get an ordinary degree, leaving more time to enjoy yourself. There is a trade-off to be made between more effort accompanied by better results, and more leisure with a poorer degree. In the end the choice has to be yours.

The advice here will work for most of the people for most of the time. You should, however, only follow a piece of advice if it works for you. Give a suggestion a fair trial before you reject it because some of the techniques require practice in order to be effective.

The word 'term' (three a year of about ten weeks each) not 'semester' (two a year of around fifteen weeks) is used throughout.

Kevin Bucknall

1
Starting Your Transition
to University Life

UNDERSTANDING THE SUCCESS FACTORS

Three elements seem to be common to those who do well at university. First, they go to all set lectures, tutorials, seminars, workshops or laboratory sessions, pay attention, and take notes. Second, they work for long hours on their own, outside the formal class time. Third, they use their time effectively. What makes them work hard is strong motivation. With a determined will to succeed you can achieve almost anything you want in life. Try to increase your motivation by regularly doing the things suggested below.

Examining your motives for going to university
A good way to start your adjustment to university life is to think about why you are going and make a list. Keep this and read it regularly to help improve your motivation.

Listing your motives
Your reasons might include one or more of the following:

- your parents, family or friends expect you to go
- your peer group are all going so you go too
- you wish to enjoy the life of a student, which sounds attractive
- you may be trying to postpone decisions about what to do with your life
- you are unable to find a job
- to gain qualifications for a particular career
- to learn about something that really interests you
- to broaden your mind and improve your quality as a human being
- you may be returning to study after some years in the work-force because you need a challenge, or you can now afford to study

11

- you seek intellectual stimulation and enjoyment.

GETTING THE FULL BENEFIT FROM UNIVERSITY

Going to university involves much personal development, and gives you the opportunity to think creatively, to learn how to organise your thoughts, and to express them clearly.

You can gain:

- **Knowledge** which consists of facts and theories. Knowledge gets out of date quickly, matters in the short term for when you are doing exams, but is probably the least important benefit in the long run.

- **Transferable skills** for your working life. These are skills that go with you and they are increasingly valued in the job market. Typically people will now switch direction several times during their working life.

The transferable skills include the ability to do the following, both quickly and effectively:

- communicate (orally and in writing)
- manage your time
- prioritise your tasks
- work in a team
- organise information
- tackle questions and problems
- analyse issues in a logical and persuasive manner.

Skills for your social and business life
- making personal friends
- a personal network of future business contacts.

Expanding your mind and developing as a human being
Major benefits of going to university include:

- mind-widening and self-discovery
- developing self-discipline and self-confidence.

Recognising that university is different from school or work

Compared with going to school
- there are no teachers to control you
- there is usually no checkup on whether you attend classes or not

- there are no parents to force you out of bed in a morning
- the freedom is great.

To an extent this can all be alarming; you are now on your own. You will learn below how to cope with the freedom.

Compared with working in a job
- there are no set hours
- there is no boss
- there is no profit and loss to worry about
- you have no regular pay packet
- there are no dress standards
- there are no office or factory politics.

The freedom can be exhilarating and you now have time to do things you want.

UNDERSTANDING WHAT GROWING UP MEANS

We all grow up as individuals with our own unique set of experiences. Growing up involves uncertainty and worry about the physical and emotional changes which occur: concern about who you are growing into; mood-swings and feelings of insecurity; concern about coping with relationships; and maybe a growing critical view of your parents and the feeling that they do not understand you.

What self-development involves

Taking responsibility for your actions
You can no longer blame others (parents, teachers, or friends) for what you do – you are now responsible for your own behaviour.

Gaining experience
Gaining experience means trying new things, but if any of these involve losing control of rational decision-taking ability, you should either avoid it or be very careful indeed. Experimenting with hard drugs, for example, can be addictive, cause personality changes, or lead to behaviour you might not normally contemplate.

Facing challenges and tackling them
If you tackle challenges successfully it is excellent, but even failure can provide a valuable learning experience, because you think about what went wrong and what you might have done to succeed.

Hard work and persistence
In life, nothing important comes without effort and you will have to work hard for what you want.

What learning about the world involves

Increasing your experiences
Going to university is a major change in your life and will provide many new experiences.

Learning from others
There is little point in reinventing the wheel. You should take the chance to study and learn from those who have gone before.

Making your own mind up about that knowledge
Not everything you read or are told is true or the whole truth. You must think about what you learn and whilst remembering it, question and criticise it.

Making adjustments in your life style
Your waking life at university will consist largely of studying, being involved in clubs or societies, and socialising.

Studying
This is your main aim – you *need* that degree – you do not get much from dropping out early or failing. You will learn how to **study** better shortly.

Clubs and societies
You will suddenly be faced with the opportunity to join lots of **clubs**. It is in your interest to join a few, perhaps a sports one for your health's sake, a social one for fun, and an intellectual or political one for interest. There will probably be one or more days where there is a 'student fair', with lots of club stalls staffed by second or third-year students trying to get you to join. Walk round and see them all before signing anything. Do this as early in the week as possible because that's when people are making new friends and forming their initial social groups.

Social life and partying
This is an important and enjoyable part of your life. You need to relax and enjoy your university life – it is the best time of life for many people. But be careful not to overdo it! You may still have to learn how much you can drink safely without suffering. If you throw up, suffer the whirling pit when you close your eyes, or cannot remember all of the

previous evening, you drank too much. Be warned! Over indulgence in alcohol is a danger in the first year and causes many to do badly.

The initial worries will quickly pass
It is normal to feel uncertain, insecure or just plain scared when you arrive at university. You do not know what it's about or what will be expected of you. Fear of the unknown can be powerful. You will probably also feel excited and exhilarated by the new opportunities. It can take a few weeks to settle down but most students manage to adapt.

If this is your first time living away from home expect to feel homesick, especially in the first week or two. If you make some new friends quickly on your first day it will help to reduce the problem. Try to persuade your parents that a telephone card would allow you to ring home more often. If you should feel a bit low, use it to call parents or a close friend – it will improve your morale.

Dealing with freedom

Choosing study rather than full-time fun
Freedom is a heady drug if you have come straight from school, particularly a boarding school where the environment is carefully controlled. At university, all restrictions are removed and the choice of how you spend your time is entirely yours. You will rarely have compulsory lectures (although this depends on your university), and you can stay in bed all morning if you wish. Be careful not to spend the bulk of the first term drinking in the union bar, playing pool, and neglecting your studies. How can you tackle this new seductive freedom? By:

- making your own weekly timetable
- making a daily list of tasks
- keeping an assignments diary
- working to increase your motivation.

Making your own weekly timetable
You can draw up a **seven-day schedule**, starting with the earliest time of day you begin studying or attending class, and covering the period until you go to bed. When you have finished, stick it on the wall or somewhere you can see it easily. On this **timetable** you might want to use different colours for lectures, tutorials, workshops, *etc* to make it easy to read at a glance.

- Did I attend all recommended lectures, tutorials and workshops, *etc*? ☐

- Am I up to date with items I have to submit? ☐

- Did I spend at least 10 minutes a day practising drawing diagrams, learning vocabulary list, formula, *etc*? ☐

- Did I get into the library to read set texts? ☐

- Did I get into the library to search for information for myself? ☐

- Did I study part of the relevant textbook in each subject? ☐

Fig. 1. A checklist of questions for the end of each week.

Contact time

In humanities and the social sciences, you might typically have eleven to thirteen hours formal contact a week, which is less than you were used to at school or at work. This teaching period is however only a fraction of the time you are expected to study. You are supposed to learn on your own. Depending on the individual, for each one hour of formal teaching you might need to do around two or three hours of personal study for decent results. In engineering and the sciences you are more likely to have a longer formal schedule to follow.

Taking time off

How many evenings you work depends in part on your personal sleep cycle: some people wake late but are prepared to study until 2 a.m. Others wake naturally around 5 a.m. and study until breakfast at about 8 a.m., which is equivalent to an evening's work on its own. A typical student who wants to do well can allow maybe two evenings a week off from study and take a day off at the weekend; those who just want a bare pass might take most evenings off as well as much of the weekend and gamble they get through. My suggestion is to err on the side of more study in the early days – it is easier to decide later to take more leisure time than to force yourself to study harder. In your non-study time, try to play a sport or engage in some very different relaxing activity.

Assessing your timetable

When you have finished your draft timetable, add up the hours – if they are less than 40 a week, you are not exactly planning to work hard. In 1993 full-time employees in Britain typically worked 43 hours a week. Try to balance your subjects so that you do not fall behind anywhere; later on you can adjust your work schedule if you find you are falling behind in a particular subject. Remember to allocate time for 'assignment research' as you will have new essays, *etc* coming up. Also, allow yourself some relaxation time each day. Making a checklist of questions to ask yourself at the end of each week will help you to make sure you are managing your time efficiently. See Figure 1.

Making a daily list of tasks
It helps if you carry a **list** of what you intend to do each day. The list should include the time and place of your lecture, tutorials, seminars, workshops or lab sessions, as well as what you will do in your personal study time. You might set aside a special half an hour for practising drawing diagrams, revising vocabulary lists or whatever your particular subject needs, some time for going over the day's notes, and say half an hour for revision of things done earlier in the term. Carry your daily list with you and don't forget to check it regularly. Cross off each item when you have done it and enjoy the feeling of achievement and success!

Keeping an assignments diary
You might find it a good idea to note in your diary when assignments are due, and also flag them early enough to prepare. Depending on your abilities and the rest of your timetable, you might need maybe three or four days for short essays and perhaps a week or two for longer items. Adjust your lead time as necessary.

Working to increase your motivation
See the section on 'strengthening your motivation and developing self-discipline' in Chapter 2 for advice on **working to increase your motivation**.

DECIDING THE ESSENTIALS: HOUSING, TRANSPORT, FOOD AND FINANCE

The housing and transport problems need tackling early while the food problem largely depends on your housing decision.

Choosing where to live

Home is the cheapest
Living at home is a good option if you get along with your family and

go to your local university. In England it used to be fashionable to go to a university in a different city but it is becoming common to go to the local university as it is cheaper. If you do this, even if you are not living at home your parents may invite you for meals, including that important Sunday lunch, and help in other ways. On the other hand, going away can be more fun and you will grow up faster.

University accommodation
University accommodation is often the best in the first year. Halls of residence are great and you have a ready-made social group. You must apply early, as soon as you know you have been accepted, and you might find that you have to move out after a year or two to make room for new first-year students. On weekdays they usually supply breakfast and an evening meal, and all three meals at the weekend. The food will not be great but it should be adequate. Petty thieving can sometimes be a problem so you should lock your door if you leave your room even briefly. University flats mean you will have to cook, maybe sharing a kitchen with a few other students. University accommodation is often located relatively close to the university and transport may be easier. It also avoids the pitfalls of private accommodation.

Private accommodation
Private accommodation is common in your second or third year and includes the choice of a bedsitter or sharing a house. Bedsitters are not the best choice for first-year students but may be easier than sharing a house. Potential bedsitter problems include:

- being located in a non-student areas (awful!)
- being with an unpleasant family (worse!)
- poor food (if supplied)
- or having to cook
- loneliness.

If you find things are not working out in your bedsitter, find alternative accommodation before you tell them you are leaving.

Sharing a house or flat is often a good bet in your second or third year when you are more experienced and you can be with friends. It may be worth paying a little extra in rent to get into a nice place in a good location where you will be happy and can get to parties *etc* easily and without huge transport costs. The larger the group, the cheaper per head, but the greater the noise and distraction.

Sharing a house or flat can have problems such as:

- Some houses and flats can be in poor condition (especially damp; bathroom/kitchen inadequate; poor electrical wiring; old and dangerous gas fires).

- Finding suitable flat-mates can be hard.

- Some people turn out to be impossible to live with and disputes arise.

- Rostered duties (cooking; cleaning) may be ignored.

- Food disappears and everyone looks innocent.

- Getting the rent and electricity share from everyone is not easy.

- The kitty for communal goods (washing-up liquid, *etc*) empties rapidly.

- The phone bill always seems to be higher than the calls people admit to making.

- The only tidy person in a house of slobs tends to do all the cleaning and tidying.

- An obsessive cleaner annoys us slobs.

- It is too easy to get distracted and not study when there are several other students around.

- The cost of setting up is high and will include a deposit and rent in advance.

- In some areas, burglars and thieves seem to target student houses.

Minimum equipment you will need for the place
Bedding, alarm clock, iron, cutlery, plates, mugs, a kettle, one or two saucepans and frying pans, cleaning materials, a bucket and a broom. You can try charity shops, car boot sales and weekend markets for second-hand serviceable stuff.

When you leave, try to get everybody to help clean the place thoroughly and make the flat or house glisten. This will substantially improve your chances of getting your deposit back.

Dealing with the problem of transport

If you don't get into university accommodation you should make sure you consider the **transport problem** when choosing where to live. Try to get on or near a public transport route that goes directly to the university – having to make a change wastes much time. Ask about public transport passes which can save a lot of money. Freshers sometimes get special deals and if you are offered one by a reliable company with good schedules, they are usually worthwhile. If you have a car, consider sharing rides and getting a contribution towards petrol and other costs – you can advertise on noticeboards around the university. To deter thieves, never leave anything visible in a car and fit an antitheft device. A visible steering wheel lock is actually not hard to deal with but it encourages the thief to move on to a different vehicle. Motorbikes are cheaper to buy and run than cars but are more dangerous. A bicycle is even cheaper and many students rely heavily on their bike, but they can also be dangerous. Buy the best lock and chain you can afford, it is cheaper than replacing your bike. You should lock your bicycle to something solid, as well as both wheels to the frame, and take all removable parts with you when you leave.

Eating cheaply

Living in a hall of residence
You will probably have to buy lunch at the university unless you have somewhere to keep food that you can make into sandwiches to take in with you (unlikely). Some students find it saves money if they force down as big a breakfast and evening meal as possible and eat little or nothing at lunchtime. It is not a good health practice but they do it anyway.

Living off campus
Eating in restaurants is not cheap and too often neither is the refectory. In particular, sausages and meat pies are rarely good value: there is relatively little meat in them, if you ignore the bits like noses, lips and ears, which makes them an unusually expensive way of buying meat. Commercial hamburgers are not particularly good value either.

It is always cheaper to buy the raw materials and cook your own food. Buy unwashed potatoes which are cheaper. Curries and vegetarian dishes using beans are nutritious and cheap to make. Leftovers make good cheap eating and if you roast or boil more potatoes than you want, you can eat them cold or fry them up later. If you roast a chicken, keep all the bones and bits of gristle from meal times and boil them up with the carcass and a vegetable and herb or two to make a great soup.

If you are new to cooking, buy a beginner's cook book and make sure it explains the terms it uses, like 'sauté' or 'parboil'. Unless you have some experience, you should avoid any book that says things like 'prepare the cabbage in the usual way...' or 'cook until tender' without indicating how long you are likely to be hanging around. Try Cas Clarke, *Grub on a Grant*, Headline, 1991, for a good start and consider the useful tips.

Do not skimp on breakfast which would reduce your energy to study and enjoy yourself. A big muesli breakfast is very filling, especially if you add some nuts and chopped up dried or fresh fruit of your own. You should buy the best muesli you can; it may look more expensive but on a per meal basis, the difference is tiny. You will not eat it if you do not like it. Adding yoghurt or honey to your dish is a good way of making a boring muesli more interesting.

Managing your finances
Other than any savings, your possible sources of money are grants, loans, parental contributions, a part-time job or, for a fortunate few, sponsorship by a company. If you are a member of a trade union, it is worth checking the rules to see if they offer any educational assistance. You can receive your full year's government grant in one lump but it is better to take a proportion each term which helps you to spread it over the year.

During the 1990s the government has increased student numbers but tried to contain educational expenditure, in part by forcing students to take more in loans rather than giving adequate grants. Most students are poor, grants are means-tested, their real value has been cut and the situation currently looks bleak. If your parents have less than £15,500 you should get a full grant; if they receive over £32,000 you will probably get nothing at all. In 1996, the full grant was only £1,885 (£2,340 in London), and even those on a full grant could not manage, particularly in London. The grant barely covers accommodation costs and it is usual to get into debt. In the mid-1990s, a typical student can expect to have a debt of around £2,300 by the time they graduate, with £938 owed to the Student Loan Company (SLC).

Borrowing
The majority of students, about 65 per cent in 1995, borrowed money. If you have to borrow, check first with the SLC as their loans are interest free until you graduate, and you get five years to repay after that if you are in a job and also earning enough. This is currently defined as 85 per cent of the average wage, working out at £15,204 in 1995. Only one in three graduates earns this in their first job. At present, there is a feeling that many loans from the SLC will never be repaid. The maximum loan in 1995 was £1,695 for those in London and living away from home, or £1,385 outside London. Living at home the maximum loan was £1,065.

You can approach a bank but overdrafts are more expensive than the SLC loans. You can also ask your university for help. It will have a government Access Account for making loans and may also have a scheme of its own from which you can borrow.

Apart from these necessary loans, if you are just starting in life, it can be a good idea to borrow a small amount from a bank, say £100, then repay it on time. If you do this once or twice, it starts to build you a good credit rating so that when you really do need money you can get it more easily.

Making a budget

You should make a **weekly budget** and try hard to stick within it. For the first month you should keep track of how you *really* spend your money as opposed to how you *plan* to. You may need to adjust your spending pattern or seek an additional income in the light of reality.

Avoiding credit cards

Never accept a **credit card** as a student. It is too dangerous a temptation to spend and you are likely to run up debts that you cannot repay. If you already have such a card, why not take a pair of scissors and cut it up? Switch cards also make it easier for you to spend and you might be better off without one. On the other hand, a cashpoint card is handy and means you can get out small amounts of money when you need it.

Getting a part-time job

You will probably need to take a vacation job to survive. During term, you might have to consider taking a **part-time job**, probably in the evenings or at the weekend. In the mid-1990s, you can expect to earn about £3.20 an hour and work ten hours a week – if you can find a job. You can ask at your student union office if they know of any firms who hire, or you can see the university employment officer. Also, talk to other students, read the adverts in the local newspaper and keep an eye open for notices in shops, café and pub windows. You can try the Employment Service Jobcentre but don't expect too much.

Living cheaply

Do *not* be a fashion victim. You are a university student, not a merchant banker, so spend as little as you can on clothes. Buy in charity shops unless you have a 'thing' about second-hand clothing. If you must have a great outfit to wear only once or twice, it is often cheaper to hire than to buy. Clothing often makes up a surprisingly high percentage of spending and offers scope for economising.

Keeping warm offers possibilities for saving. In winter, it is cheaper to wear more clothes (several layers work best) or do a bit of exercise than turn up the central heating or switch on an electric fire. The university library is also a warm place to be and you can study comfortably there.

Try to find free or cheap entertainment where possible. Listening to the radio and watching TV is free once you have a set and licence. Your hall of residence probably has a TV. If sharing a house, somebody's parents might be persuaded to give you their old set and buy themselves a new one. Check the student and local newspaper for free entertainments that you can travel to cheaply. Figure 2 offers a few more ideas for living cheaply.

Mature students

Mature students often have other financial commitments over and above day-to-day living expenses, the following are some ways of helping with these:

- If you have dependent children you can claim benefits from the state while you are at university.

- If you are paying off a mortgage, think about changing to a fixed interest payment for your three years at university, as this will reduce your outlay.

- Have you a marketable skill that will allow you to earn part-time?

- Can you get a part-time job somewhere you worked before?

- Do you have any relatives or other contacts who can offer you work?

USING FRESHER WEEK TO GOOD ADVANTAGE

Surviving your first day

Registration as a student and getting your student card are really all that matter on your first day. The rest largely consists of you hanging about waiting for things to happen and being talked at by a variety of people. Usually not a lot of what you are told is truly important, but take a notepad and pen to write down anything that you might want to remember. The best reason for going is to make friends when standing in queues or sitting around. On your first evening you have to meet with friends and do something, so set up an appointment during the day with a few people. If you are in university accommodation, sitting with your door open attracts casual callers and helps you meet people. Whatever happens, *do not stay home alone on your first evening* – this is important! There might be a dance organised, or a film show; if you do not hear about anything special, you can try the student union where you are guaranteed to meet people.

Using the rest of fresher week

Use any spare time to find out where things are: the student union and

TIPS FOR CHEAP LIVING

☐ If you have a hobby, put it aside for your university years.

☐ Turn off the lights when not in the room to save electricity.

☐ Avoid ordering delivered pizza and other foods, there is always a delivery charge.

☐ A small joint is easy to roast and you can get several meals off one.

☐ Buy in cheap supermarkets but ignore the impulse items by the till.

☐ Buy supermarket food on special offer but check it is not past its 'use-by date'.

☐ Do not go fun shopping and try to buy only what you desperately need rather than simply want.

☐ Avoid the shopping sales.

☐ Never buy something just because it looks cheap, unless you were planning to buy it anyway at a higher price.

☐ If you have a fridge, decide what you want before you open the door.

☐ Dishwashers are costly to use and washing up by hand is far cheaper.

☐ Drinks can be expensive at university. If you carry a small screw top water bottle you can refill it at a tap for free.

Fig. 2. Ideas for living cheaply.

what is in it; the refectory; all the other eating and coffee places; the bookshop, bank, post office or whatever commercial shops there are; and the library. If you are new in town, look at a map and learn your way around. It is useful to know the local entertainment possibilities, including cafés and pubs. You can also check out the transport system and bus routes, try and get a bus map, and find out about the last bus or late night service. You will need some kind of bag to carry your books and notes around but don't rush out and buy that expensive briefcase immediately. A free supermarket bag will do for a few days until you see what the current fashion is. Similarly, if you are given reading lists this early, do not race out and buy all the books suggested. You will probably not need to own them all (see the section on 'using your set textbook to the best advantage' in Chapter 3).

It is useful to look at the latest university handbook and read the general information section – it will answer some of your questions and help to ease your passage into this new and exciting life. The university library will have a copy available for you to borrow – it isn't worth buying.

Socialising

University is primarily for you to learn and be taught, but also to have fun. Use this first week to make friends and start to build a social group for when the studying and learning begin. Try to get to the organised entertainment like discos or student hops that are held during this week.

CASE STUDIES

Let us introduce three students of different backgrounds and abilities who we will follow in subsequent chapters. Each has strengths and weaknesses in their period of adjustment to university life.

Alan Thompson needs less out of fresher week
Alan is 32 years old, lives with his spouse and spent a year living and working abroad, so he has fewer problems of adjusting to new circumstances. He goes to all the introductory sessions and joins three clubs (drama, squash and film). He is a bit worried about whether he can afford university but he is confident he will succeed. He didn't participate in many fresher week activities, because he has a wife and outside friends, and isn't seeking a social life in the university.

Jane Richards' social life doesn't look promising
Jane is 19 years old and living with her parents. She is generally unassertive, slow to make friends, and often tends to feel a bit out of things. She is intelligent and hard working but still worries about

succeeding. She spent a year working in a bank before she came to university but made few friends. She went straight home after registration ended and sat reading the bumf she had been given. During the week she finds out where everything is, but she doesn't join any clubs so that socially she is already not getting as much as she could out of university.

Bob Jones' social life is already looking good

Bob is 18 years old, came straight from school and manages to get into a hall of residence. He joins six clubs on the first day (including a boozing group); this is his first taste of freedom and he is determined to enjoy it – and is already on the track to wasting time. On the first night he goes to a dance at the university where he drinks a lot and wipes himself out but already he knows a dozen people and has picked up an invitation to a party next weekend.

DISCUSSION POINTS

1. Are your reasons for going to university the same as your friends'? Are your reasons associated with strong motivation?
2. What sort of job do you hope to do and what skills (as opposed to knowledge) would help you to succeed in it?
3. How many hours do your parents work in a week? How does this compare with your timetable?

SUMMARY

- A strong will to succeed is important; try to do things to increase it.
- Those who do well go to all the sessions, study on their own, and use their time effectively.
- You will need to adjust your life style at university.
- The sudden freedom can be hard to cope with.
- Excessive drinking and socialising are dangers.
- Your initial worries and uncertainty will quickly pass.
- Sort out your housing and transport problems early.
- Adjust your behaviour in order to live cheaply.
- Join a few clubs at once and make friends as fast as you can.
- Do not stay in alone on your first evening at university.

2
Understanding What is
Expected of You

GRASPING WHAT A UNIVERSITY IS

Your university has only two main functions. These are to pass on existing knowledge to a new generation so that nothing is forgotten, and to push back the frontiers of knowledge. In simpler words, it is responsible for teaching and research. A third function has begun to emerge since the 1980s – consultancy. Academics are now expected to bring in extra money for the university, as governments become stingier.

Seeing how your department fits into the university

The organisation of the university
Most universities have a similar structure but may use slightly different names. At the very top is a governing body, often called a **senate** or **council**, that is legally responsible for the whole institution. It meets perhaps once a month for maybe three hours. There is usually a **chancellor** whose function is largely honorary but carries great prestige. The person who really runs the place is the **vice-chancellor**. He is 'Mister Big' and you will probably never meet yours. Below him are several **deans** who are each in charge of a **faculty**, which is a grouping of similar disciplines. Under that level there will be several **departments**, each with its own departmental head. In newer universities there may be **schools** either under the faculty level, or sometimes replacing it.

The faculty side
The people who teach and do research are called **faculty staff**. At the top are **professors**, followed by **associate professors** or **readers**, then **senior lecturers, lecturers, assistant lecturers** and maybe **teaching assistants**. A department head might be a professor, senior lecturer or even perhaps a lecturer. **Doctors** are people who have earned a PhD. Unless told otherwise, you should address professors and associate professors as 'Professor X' and anyone else with a doctorate as 'Doctor X'.

The administrative side
The administration runs the university for the staff and students. At the top is the **registrar** who controls all the various functional departmental chiefs who are in charge of keeping the place clean, running the library and refectory, paying the staff salaries and so forth.

KNOWING WHAT YOU ARE SUPPOSED TO DO

Gaining knowledge and developing skills
First, you will gain knowledge and develop skills through a relatively small number of formal teaching sessions. You spend a lot more time going off to learn informally on your own or with others.

Assessment
Second, you are assessed to check that you have reached an acceptable level. You do written essays, present oral assignments, sit exams and the like. When you are thought to be good enough you are given a degree. For most it is a Bachelor of Arts (BA) or Bachelor of Science (BSc) and it normally takes three years, although four year degrees are coming in.

Most students in England do an honours degree, and get one of the following levels:

- First class (a first)
- Upper second class (a two-one)
- Lower second class (a two-two)
- Pass
- Fail.

Above this first degree level, there is the Master of Arts (MA) or Master of Science (MSc) which takes a year or two; the Masters can be done by pure research (Mres) which involves writing a major dissertation. Above this level is the Doctor of Philosophy (PhD) which few bother to do unless going to work in universities. It is a pure research degree (but with some course work in the USA), and must make an original contribution to knowledge; while normally financed for three years it often takes considerably more to finish. The degree of Doctor of Science (DS) may be awarded to a few scientists, based purely upon their published articles and books.

Formal teaching sessions
For the formal learning time you have to:

- attend various teaching sessions (lectures, tutorials, *etc*), listen and take notes

- submit some written assignments (essays, quizzes, tests, *etc*)
- present some oral assignments (tutorial or seminar papers, project reports, or role-playing presentations).

Informal learning
In the informal learning time you must:

- read books and journal articles, and take notes in the library
- read and learn the notes you have taken
- discuss, debate and argue passionately with anybody you can find.

Reading the information supplied
You will settle down quicker if you read what you are given. Much of what may puzzle you at first is often described in handouts – the trouble is, however, that you get so many you may either not read them, or forget what is in them. When you have a question, it is a good idea to check first to see if one of these handouts has already given you the answer.

Attending lectures, tutorials, seminars, workshops and lab sessions

Lectures
Lectures are designed to pass information to you in an efficient way. They can be quite large events, in the first year especially, so you should not be surprised if there are several hundred fellow students present. In your first year lectures may consist largely of mainstream knowledge but in the second and third year they often contain more original information. Lectures do not often blindly follow the textbook and you might find the set text being criticised. You may be allowed to ask questions in lectures and if you are not clear whether this is the case you should ask. You will need to take notes.

Tutorials
Tutorials are small groups with one staff member and up to half a dozen students – probably a student reads out a short essay paper they have prepared, and you write down any questions and comments which you would like to ask during the following discussion. The tutor leads the discussion and might sum up. The purpose of tutorials is to encourage you to think for yourself, discuss what you have heard, criticise views, and put ideas into context. One-staff-to-one-student tutorials are becoming a definite luxury these days.

Seminars
Seminars are usually given to larger groups than tutorials, but work in a similar although perhaps more formal way.

Workshops and lab sessions
Workshops vary in how they operate, but the constant factor is that you do something rather than sit and listen. You may have to do mathematical exercises, answer multiple choice questions, participate in small group discussions of previously assigned materials, engage in role-playing, or work with apparatus. There are many things that can be done in workshops, depending on the subject being studied. You will receive help from the member of staff present who will tell you what to do and then let you loose. Lab sessions are common in science, engineering and psychology and similarly require effort from you, often working with apparatus or observing.

Research indicates that people who interact with information and actively do something remember up to four times as much as they do if they are simply told. The message is you should always go to workshops and tutorials and participate strongly.

Learning your notes
Notes are of no value until you read them. It is no good taking them and filing them away to be forgotten. You should read your notes regularly and revise, learning as you go.

MAKING ADJUSTMENTS TO HELP YOU STUDY

Building a network of friends and support groups
A network of friends and support groups is essential if you are to adapt to university life quickly, enjoy yourself, avoid loneliness, and banish feelings of depression or homesickness. You cannot study properly if suffering emotional upsets. You might already know some people who came to university with you and who will provide a nucleus of friends. However, you will keep meeting people and develop new friends, so that as time passes you might find you drift away from the original ones.

Finding a study-buddy
A **study-buddy** is virtually essential for easy and enjoyable learning. Working alone in individual competition has been traditionally regarded as normal at university but you can do much better if you find a friend with whom to work closely. You will settle down more quickly and learn more easily if you find a good study-buddy (a naff phrase but an invaluable help). You should try to find someone

congenial early (see the section on 'Learning with a study-buddy or study group' in Chapter 3).

Study groups can be even more useful. They comprise of a set of like-minded people who get along and are doing the same course. They meet together and help each other learn. It is strongly recommended that you join such a group.

DEALING WITH PROBLEMS

Academic problems

If you find you are not keeping up with the work, failing to read the assigned material, not getting essays in on time and the like, then examine your conscience. Have you been lazy? (be honest!) If so, the solution is simple: work harder. You probably need to reduce your leisure activities, increase your total work hours, and perhaps reallocate your time on your weekly list towards a subject in which you are falling behind. You should definitely try to work more efficiently too. Try the techniques described in Chapters 3 and 4 below. If you have not got one yet, find a study-buddy, or join/start a study group.

Financial and personal problems

You should always seek help with financial and personal problems. Just telling someone about it can help and bring great relief: the religious confessional and psychiatrist's couch have long provided peace of mind to many.

Your problems may fall into areas such as financial, emotional, social, family, or be connected with health or drugs. Frequently there will be a mixture of several problems because they often tend to reinforce each other.

Seeking advice
You can get advice from:

- your personal tutor
- your university student counselling service or welfare officer (the name varies)
- the university health service nurse or doctor
- the student union
- your partner (if you have one)
- personal friends and support groups
- your local religious leader (if a member of a religion)
- your parents (if your relationship permits)
- your bank manager (financial).

Dealing with the advice
You should not just accept the first advice offered but think it over. It pays to get suggestions from more than one source and compare what you have been told. In the end you must make your own decision as a responsible adult.

Coping with sexual harassment
It is sometimes hard to recognise sexual harassment: physical touching, stroking and patting are easy to identify, as is verbal abuse. Some jokes and language used may qualify as harassment. It is a rapidly changing and difficult area – values are in the process of altering, and not everyone accepts the same set, particularly if from a different age group or culture.

My personal views are that telling you that you are pretty, handsome, sexy, *etc* is not harassment, it is only 'an offer to treat' (as lawyers say with unconscious irony) and helps to keep the human race going. Harassment seems to involve repetition and a refusal to stop after you have said no or otherwise made it clear that you do not welcome the approach. If you are not sure if you are being harassed, go and talk to someone about it. You can ask in your departmental office if your university has a sexual harassment officer, ask at the student union office, check with the women's group (if you are female) or talk to the people at your university medical centre.

Do not forget that you can be sexually harassed by someone of the same sex.

Coping with stress
There are many ways of coping with stress. If you have a religious belief it can offer consolation and help reduce the level of stress. Physical exercise is a good way of releasing tension, and yoga is particularly helpful. Various schools of meditation offer ways of reducing stress. You can try the relaxation techniques described in Chapter 6.

ADJUSTING TO UNIVERSITY LIFE

Coming straight from school
Your main problem in the first year is likely to be coping with the freedom. Ways of dealing with this were discussed in Chapter 1 on page 15.

Another short-term problem might well be the uncertainty that you may feel as you face the flood of new experiences. It is part of growing up to deal with uncertainty and learn from your experiences and mistakes. Remember that you are not alone and everyone around you faces the same dilemmas, however well they may hide their fears. Although the initial newness fades quickly, the whole of the first year is in some way new, and the feelings of excitement and confusion may linger on for some time. You should try to see your time at university as an immense and exciting opportunity, as well as a challenge, and something you enjoy as you grapple with and surmount problems.

Dealing with bad study habits
At school, if you did not like a particular teacher you probably found that subject boring, you may have blocked the information being given to you and did not work hard at the subject. Conversely, if you liked the teacher, you probably did well at that subject. From now on you have no teachers, only lecturers and tutors of some kind and personal liking or disliking is no longer relevant.

Some students develop another bad habit at school – they butter up and flatter teachers in order to improve their standing and get better marks. If you found this a fast track to success, be aware that those days are gone. Only good written and oral assignments and exam results count now.

A different wile at school is to find out who will mark the paper and then write the answer you believe that teacher expects. Goodbye to all that! Favouritism and conformity rarely count at university. In many courses, especially in large first-year classes, you will not even know who will mark your assignment.

Another unhelpful attitude involves trying to measure success by the degree of effort that went into an assignment, rather than the quality of the output. It is never any use at university appealing a grade on the grounds you spent six weeks working hard on it. That is irrelevant.

Adjustment for the mature student

Boosting your self-confidence
You might feel insecure and uncertain, surrounded by all these bright eager youngsters. You might feel you have been away too long and forgotten how to study. No problem! This book tells you how. You *can* get a degree; all you need is confidence and hard work – but you might have to keep reminding yourself of that. Age is not a barrier to learning and, although it is bit harder to learn at 50 years of age that it is at 15, it isn't that much harder. People who go to university after they have been away from school score better on average than those who go straight from school. Don't be afraid that you will be alone. Unless you are very unlucky there should be people around your age – mature students increasingly attend university.

Some mature students fear that they will look foolish or lose face by expressing a wrong opinion. If you have been housebound for years, you may feel afraid to join in discussions or say what you think in case you are laughed at. Try to fight this feeling. You are more likely to find that the younger students take your word more seriously just because you are older and more experienced. They are often rather frightened of you, but will rarely admit it.

As a mature student you will have many strengths – read on and you will begin to recognise them.

Maturity
Your greater age means that your attitudes are more mature and you are likely to make quicker and better decisions than young people. Also you are not still growing up, or subject to hormone changes that can produce sudden swings in emotions and moods, nor are you worried about the changes in your body and feelings. You might no longer be in the grip of an intense sexual drive and are probably not spending so much time dreaming about or pursuing those elusive partners.

Motivation
You will be a lot more motivated to succeed than many youngsters: you really want to get that degree, you know what you are giving up in terms of income, and are aware of the costs in family terms. All this means you will be motivated to work harder and this is often worth more than youthful exuberance.

Experience and skills
You are probably able to notice interlinkages and causes and effects more easily than the less experienced. On average, you will also have better communication skills, particularly in speaking, and be generally more poised. You have had the rough corners knocked off, survived office politics or factory humour, and perhaps coped with the rearing of children. A major plus is that the experience and wider information you possess provide hooks on which you can easily hang new knowledge and learn easily.

Sources of information you may have open to you
You have a depth of experience that can help you immensely when faced with new ideas and knowledge; many propositions that can startle an 18-year-old may seem commonplace to you. You are also likely to have more friends and relatives with different experiences that you can call on for help or with whom you can discuss issues.

A supportive partner
You are more likely to have a supportive partner than the typical 18-

year-old and that can be a big help in allowing you time to study and increasing your motivation.

Financial security
You will probably be more financially secure than those coming straight from school, which means that you may not need to take a part-time job to supplement your income. If you have to work, you will probably earn more per hour and perhaps not have to work as long. You can also afford to buy the textbooks and other recommended material, whereas some of the young students may be forced to go without or have to share with others.

Despite the advantages you possess, there are a few special areas that you might have to work at.

Coping with a lower standard of living
Your income will be less, perhaps substantially so, and it can be painful to reduce your standard of living. You may have to give up eating out, and severely curtail spending on clothes and entertainment. You may have to give up smoking and limit your consumption of wine and spirits. It will hurt at first – keep telling yourself the sacrifice will be worth it and think of the future jobs you will be eligible for.

Fighting feelings of inadequacy
Do not worry about any feelings of inadequacy or fear that you will be unable to get a degree. Keep telling yourself you will do it and remind yourself of your advantages. Don't worry that you have forgotten how to study and have been away too long – you will be rusty but your essential skill has not gone – it is like riding a bicycle, you can still do it but it takes a bit of practice to do it well again.

Avoiding monopolising discussions
If you happen to be one of the extrovert and self-assured mature students, be careful not to monopolise discussions as this tends to annoy people. A good group leader should prevent this, but young tutors often lack experience and if younger than you they may find it hard to reign you in. Be aware that you can get a bad reputation for continually saying 'When I worked in . . .', and telling strings of anecdotes.

Finding a study-buddy
It will help you if you seek out someone about your own age with whom you can work and discuss your concerns. You are looking for a good, compatible study-buddy, not someone who whinges and complains – you need support, not membership of a mutual moaning society.

Coping with computers
If you were educated before the widespread availability of personal computers you may well be afraid of them. Don't be! They are fast, stupid toys that are great fun as well as tremendous help. You can learn to use one. Most academics are old enough not to have been brought up with computers and they managed to learn. You need one for word processing (writing and printing) your assignments.

Learning by doing
To cope with the brain finding it slightly harder to learn new things as you get older, you can compensate by actively doing things as part of your learning process, rather than simply reading. To widen your approach, try:

- condensing your notes regularly

- making your notes distinctive by adding colour or even small cartoons

- practising drawing diagrams, figures, *etc* from your textbook and lectures

- making up your own tables of relationships, *etc* from the textbook and lectures

- going to search in the library for your own information for a set period each day

- going through different textbooks and comparing explanations of the same point

- meeting daily with your study-buddy to explain what you have learned

- telling your partner what each lecture was about.

Sorting out your family relationships
This should be a main priority because a supportive partner will make learning a lot easier. Before you start at university, sit and discuss who will do what, *eg* pick up the children, cook the meals, wash up, shop, and clean the house. It might help if you make a roster so it is clear who does what and when.

Despite your best efforts, you may have to cope with feelings of resentment from your family if you stay up half the night to finish an essay then sleep in the next day, particularly if you were rostered for some task. It is imperative that you avoid letting things fester. You could choose to set aside time, say every Sunday evening, to discuss how things are going, what irritates the others, and decide what adjustments can be made to put things right. Keeping the family happy, or at least out of revolt mode, is essential.

The possibility of shortening your course
With your experiences, you might find some of them can gain you credit towards a degree, which means you could finish more quickly. Things like setting up and running a business, working in a foreign country, managing a department, or gaining professional qualifications might help you. It is worth asking in your departmental office if they have any special awards of credit along such lines, you might get lucky.

STRENGTHENING YOUR MOTIVATION

Increasing your motivation and developing self-discipline is central to success. You can:

- Consciously fight the cunning suggestions your brain will throw up that it would be nice to watch TV, go for a drink, or do anything rather than be forced into studying.

- Remind yourself constantly of your reasons for coming to university – keep reading the list you made in Chapter 1.

- Look at your weekly timetable and tell yourself how much you look forward to various periods of study.

- Think of the good job you hope to get when you finish your degree.

- Reflect how much university life is better than school/work and you want to stay in it.

- Consider what it is costing you to be at university in terms of money and time – and the need not to waste it.

- Reflect on the shame if you fail, and have to go home and confess to friends and family.

- Work with a study-buddy or group on a regular basis.

- Put up little notes where you can see them, like 'Work!', 'Only eight weeks to the exams!', or whatever might help you.

CASE STUDIES

Alan's age and experience helps swift adaptation
Alan is starting to fit in well – by the end of the first month his wife accepts his busy study periods but gets irritated now and then, especially as he is already cast in a play and rehearsing two evenings a week and Saturday afternoons. They have discussed the problem and agree that he is responsible for preparing the Sunday dinner to compensate. He has sold his car and bought a bike which he uses to get

to and from university and takes sandwiches to the university for lunch, both of which save money.

The academic work is going well, but...

Jane is not making many friends and is not as happy as she could be, however, she finds it difficult to discuss the problem with her parents. She is studying hard and enjoying the academic challenge. She spends most evenings in the library or working at home and even reads over her notes while sitting on the bus. She takes her lunch in, but treats herself to lunch on a Friday. Her parents help out with money if she needs anything badly enough.

Freedom can go to the head

Bob is making heaps of friends but the freedom is going to his head and he is drinking too much too often. He never works in the evenings and is often out with friends or in the union bar. He walks to the hall of residence. He does not eat lunch but has a couple of pints in the university most days. He has found his grant is disappearing rapidly and has been forced to get a job behind the bar in a local pub working two evenings a week.

DISCUSSION POINTS

1. Are you happy using a computer for word processing? Does your university allow you access to computers attached to a printer? Where are they located?

2. At school, what subjects did you do well at? Did you like the teacher? Did you do well in any subject where you did not like the teacher? What is the message?

3. Why is it undesirable to lie in bed all morning? Is it always a bad idea?

SUMMARY

- You need to spend more time studying on your own than in set sessions.
- Find a congenial person and become study-buddies.
- Join or start a study group.
- Seek help if you have problems.
- If you are straight from school, the sudden freedom can prove difficult.
- Mature students have several advantages and do better on average.
- If you are a mature student, self-confidence and family problems may need special attention.

3
Improving Your Learning Skills

Learning is an active process – you learn by going off and reading on your own, discovering information, deciding what you think and applying your knowledge to problems. You can learn a lot from arguing with other students too. From your perspective, teaching is a passive thing that the staff do to you while you sit and listen. At university you are expected to spend more time learning on your own than being taught by others. Sharpening your learning skills as early as possible can save you time and improve your marks.

UNDERSTANDING WHAT YOU ARE TRYING TO DO

When trying to grasp a new idea, theoretical model, or new information generally:

- first, you try to understand it
- second, you learn it
- third, you try to criticise it, but only after you understand it
- fourth, you try to think of any questions it raises or has left unanswered
- fifth, you try to put it into perspective and reach some conclusion.

You should always read critically, but remember, don't criticise what you can't understand.

MAKING LEARNING EASIER

There are lots of things that you can do to make learning at university easier. A central element is boosting your will to succeed (see the section on 'Strengthening your motivation and developing self-discipline' in Chapter 2). Before starting each new task, such as reading your textbook, tell yourself a few times 'I will enjoy this and I want to do it well'. This simple act may sound a trifle odd but it can help.

Early reinforcement

As soon as is practical, read over any notes you have taken that day from lectures or other sources. Such early reinforcement embeds the new information more quickly.

Making the effort to begin studying

If you are finding it hard to settle down to study, you might be able to ease yourself in and develop enthusiasm by doing some simple study-related task first. You could, for instance, file yesterday's lecture notes, sharpen your pencils, or sort out your bag. There are many such tasks that can help to nudge your mind towards study mode. The important thing is to start and do something and not sit thinking you cannot be bothered.

Reading your notes regularly

Late in each day you should try to read over the notes you took earlier that day. It will also help if you go back and read over some notes from earlier in the term. It is a good idea to set aside some time for this purpose, perhaps half an hour or so.

Explaining what you have recently read to another

This is an excellent practice because knowing you will have to explain it to your study-buddy later concentrates the mind wonderfully at the time and increases your motivation. At explanation time, you will discover your weak spots and be able to plug the holes, while the discussion with your buddy will reinforce the information.

Condensing your notes

Gathering together all your notes on one topic, reading them over, and then condensing them down is a good way of ensuring you see the outline of the topic and can identify many of its elements. The process itself is valuable and as a bonus you get an excellent summary that you can use when revising for exams.

Organising your time well

Time flies by quickly and so you might as well make the best use of it. You need to break up your activities into manageable blocks of time. Few people can concentrate fully for an hour without a break, and for some it can be as short as 25 minutes. Two study blocks of 30 minutes with 5 minutes off between, followed by a 15 minute break to do something completely different, might work for you. In the break try things like weeding the garden, making coffee, tidying your bedroom, washing up, doing the Canadian 5BX exercises, or taking a brisk walk. Then you go back refreshed to studying again. Experiment and decide what size time blocks fit you best, then organise your learning schedule to match.

You might also consider which is the best time to study for you. Some people are morning people and do good work then; others work better at night. Everyone has a time of day when their attention and ability to concentrate are weak so try to plan your leisure for your naturally slack periods.

Using those odd bits of leftover time

Everyone has small periods of time that seem too short to start something new. They might be 10 minutes or more and there can be a lot of them in the day. They may arise at any time, *eg* waiting for a meal or sitting around after you've eaten, waiting for a train, travelling by bus, or filling in time before the next lecture. These incredibly useful periods of time are too often wasted. You can use them profitably for reading the notes you took earlier in the day, reading your condensed notes from something studied earlier in the term, planning an answer to one or two questions in your textbook, looking at an existing skeleton outline and trying to improve it, or maybe going through vocabulary flash cards if you are studying a language. You might find that choosing an unusual place to do this is particularly beneficial and helps you remember – try leaning against the front door, sitting on a (strong!) coffee table, or lying down in the hallway. If you find it works for you, do it!

Finding a good place to study

Work out where you study best and try to get there. Some people like a clean desk with nothing on it but the notes they are using while others like clutter; some like sitting in an armchair with stuff piled around, others concentrate best when lying on the floor. You might like total quiet, or find you do better with background music playing. Set the conditions to suit yourself. Be careful not to get too intense and feel you can only study when wearing a particular set of clothes and with Oasis playing at full volume on the hi-fi or you will seriously limit your ability to study.

Practising questions from textbooks and study guides

Many textbooks include questions at the end of each chapter that provide you with the opportunity to practise preparing answers. If a study guide accompanies your textbook it is a good source of questions. Never waste time writing out the answer in full unless you wish to practise your writing skills, but instead make a skeleton outline.

Read the question carefully and think about it. Does it naturally divide up into sections? If so, put these down and you have a start on a skeleton outline. You could then add what you can remember about the topic. After that put down what you personally think. You might then like to read the relevant bit of the textbook and expand your skeleton answer. Later in the term you can add even more – see Chapter 5 on 'gathering the information'.

Don't worry if early in the term you cannot answer some textbook questions as you will probably cover the material later. Keep your skeleton answers and file them with your notes on the topic – they make excellent revision material.

Practising skeleton answers not only reinforces your knowledge and helps you to learn, you also develop a valuable skill. In the exam room you will need to plan skeleton answers quickly; and after you leave university you will probably need to devise fast logical responses to problems at work.

Going through old exam papers

Try to get hold of old exam papers – some universities will sell them to you but you might find the library holds a full set anyway. You can use these like textbook questions to prepare your skeleton answers. You can also try to 'spot' hot topics that come up more often than others, and concentrate your studies slightly more in those areas. Do not totally neglect areas that have not been asked about recently – there is always a first time! You may also need that information in your second or third year in other courses.

Paying attention to comments on essays

When an essay comes back don't quickly look up the mark and then file it away. The comments you get are far more valuable to you than a mere mark – they show you where you can improve. When you have had a few essays back, it is a good idea to sit and look over all the comments; if you find you are getting similar remarks it tells you that here is an area to concentrate upon. Check the comments you get against the list of common mistakes in Chapter 7, 'Essay tips – things to avoid'.

Stopping when you are tired

If you are studying and suddenly find that you are falling asleep, stop and take a break of at least 15 minutes. Remember you are trying to maximise your **learning** not just the quantity of time spent doing it. During your break, use one of the relaxation techniques (see the section in Chapter 6 on coping with nerves and learning to relax) or take a snooze if necessary. Remember to go back to studying afterwards.

Avoiding lunchtime drinking

Alcohol at lunchtime might seem attractive but it lowers your productivity and tends to make you sleepy when you are trying to study. Save your drinking for the evening if you can.

LEARNING WITH A STUDY-BUDDY OR STUDY GROUP

A study-buddy is someone doing the same course as you with whom you cooperate to help you study and learn. **A good study-buddy is the fast track to learning.**
With your study-buddy you can:

- compare and discuss your notes from the same lecture
- explain the main points of the lecture to each other
- go through the details of the lecture and see how they fit together
- before a lecture talk over what you think it will cover (read the assigned textbook chapter first)
- read the same section of the textbook and explain it to each other or quiz each other on it
- take opposing views on any questions for discussion, or papers you have to write, and argue
- pool the information you have discovered about an assignment
- share the photocopying costs of material you need
- revise jointly for exams, and test each other
- compare your skeleton outlines to the same answer.

Working in a study group
A study group is comprised of about four to six people who get together to cooperate and learn more easily, quickly and enjoyably. Such a group can be enjoyable, and immensely helpful in helping you learn.

Setting up the group
If you can, it is easier to join an existing group. If not you can set up your own by asking a few people who seem interested in the course. It is best to do this personally because advertising on a board probably won't work: you might feel foolish, may be criticised by some of the heartier brethren, and the chances are you will attract some people you cannot work with.

Trying rotating the leadership
With a small group you may not need a formal leader and can just meet

and work together when convenient. Yet there is benefit in having a leader. It makes more efficient use of the limited time – people know when to meet, why they are there, and what they will do with the session. This allows them to prepare in advance. If you rotate the leadership, everyone gets a chance to learn skills (organising, persuading; motivating; group dynamics, *etc*) and you can put it on your curriculum vitae (CV) which can help when you are looking for your first job. Employers are impressed by such things and it gives you something valuable to talk about at the interview. Rotating the leadership also prevents one person from dominating too much.

Benefiting from your study group
You can do everything you can do with your study-buddy, and more. You can:

- share the cost of textbooks – you each need the basic one but supplementary texts and other useful books can be bought and circulated within the group
- search for information as a team
- divide up the members to research into particular tutorial or seminar questions and report back
- find more material by searching in a greater number of journals
- divide up and go to different libraries to search for information
- brainstorm ideas about the answer to a question
- engage in projects as a team
- play useful learning games.

Some learning games for the study group
1. Who can recall the most from the recent lecture or last week's lecture?

2. Who can say the most about a particular topic in the course?

3. Choose a topic, and one person argues for, another against, for five minutes then the group discusses.

4. Take a question and go round in turn, everyone having to say something about it.

5. Take a question, set a time limit for each person to produce a skeleton answer; these are then circulated and discussed.

6. Divide into two teams and argue the case for and against a proposition or question.

Note: If you work on an assignment as a group, it is best to restrict it to searching for information and then discussing it. It is wise not to plot out your answer together because if you do it might lead to a subsequent charge of plagiarism if the individual essays look much alike.

USING YOUR SET TEXTBOOK TO THE BEST ADVANTAGE

Buying your main text
You generally need to own a copy of the main set textbook but you can often buy one second-hand which will be cheaper. Check the noticeboards. Make sure you get the current edition otherwise any page and chapter references given in lectures will not fit. Buy a study guide too if there is one and work through it on your own, with your study-buddy, or in your study group. A study group can share the cost of a study guide by buying perhaps only one for every two people. If there is a computer disc that comes with the textbook and you have access to a machine, it is very helpful to work through the program. It provides useful self-paced learning and lets you steadily revise material covered earlier. The computer program also lets you see another version of the material and probably has exercises to reinforce what you are learning.

Coping with lengthy book lists
You do not usually need to buy everything on the list. Some items will be good for only a small part of your course, while others may be out of date and no one has bothered to remove them. You may be able to use the library copies until you are certain what you need to buy. When you are presented with a long list, you might start by reading the most recent item on it, because it will have fewer out-of-date theories and probably contain more recent data.

Highlighting your own textbook
It is usually not the best use of your time to take notes from your set textbook. It is better to highlight it and read those bits often. If as a child you were taught it was a crime to write in books – forget it! With few exceptions, a book is not a unique work of art and the bookshop can get you dozens of identical copies if you want. The only thing

against highlighting is that it reduces the second-hand value of the book when you come to sell it later. Remember though that your goal is to learn quickly and easily, not to maximise the value of old books. When highlighting, be careful not to go through marking everything, for there is no point.

Choosing 'the best' textbook

The textbook was set because someone thought it was generally the best for that course. However, you might find that it is difficult to learn from, perhaps because it has a jocular or boring style. You should try other textbooks in the library to see if they explain things in a way that you understand better. To choose a supplementary text suitable for you, look up your textbook in the library catalogue and locate it on the shelf, then examine the books around it. Look up an issue that you know a bit about and see how each book covers it. Then borrow and use the one that you find the easiest to understand. You can also ask in your study group what others think about different textbooks. Be aware that the staff are often not a good source of information on textbooks because they do not know what particular difficulties you face nor do they sit and read textbooks much.

Finding what you need to know

When you have a topic you want to know about, start by examining the contents page – there might be a whole section or even chapter about it. If your need is specific and narrow, go to the index at the back and look it up. If you find several references, start with the marked range (*eg* 'pp. 56–64') which is likely to be central, whereas 'p. 112' may be just a passing reference.

Making notes from journals

Photocopying
Read the article through before making a decision to photocopy. If there is much that you need, and perhaps tables of data, a photocopy might be a good idea. If you only need a part of the article then taking notes is a cheaper and often better option. Please remember the copyright laws.

Reading and highlighting
Possessing a photocopy or carrying it around does not improve your learning at all. You have to read, highlight (or underline) and remember what is in your photocopies.

Colour coding
Some students find it helpful to use, say, yellow paper for the notes taken privately from journal articles, books, *etc*, and ordinary white paper for notes taken from formal lectures and the like. This can be of value if when revising you can force yourself to read a bit further than you otherwise would and finish the yellow pages too – on the other hand you may find it more trouble that it is worth.

File your notes by topic
It usually works best to file your notes (whatever their source) by topic so that you can look up or revise everything you want easily. Some students find keeping their main lecture notes separate works best for them; try it and see which you prefer.

READING EFFICIENTLY

Always read for study purposes with a pen and paper at hand. As you read, an idea might pop into your head. Ideas are valuable currency at university and you cannot afford to forget any, so write them down at once. The habit is useful for developing your ability to think and criticise.

Efficient reading means you ought to read different things at different speeds because you are reading for different reasons, so do not be concerned if the textbook seems painfully slow going. The following reading material should be read at different speeds:

Newspapers – you may only glance at the headlines, and read only a few items properly.
Escapist paperbacks – you should read these rapidly.
Good novels – these should be read relatively slowly.
Textbooks – should be read the slowest of all.

Using different approaches
The **intro-conclusion** approach is useful with journal articles. When reading an article, if often helps if you first read the introduction, then jump to the conclusion to get the gist of the paper – then go back and read it properly.

The SQ3R sequence approach
The SQ3R sequence approach is useful for larger texts and involves five stages:

1. *Survey*   You first skim through, reading only the headings, sub-

headings and anything in upper-case, bold or italic print. This gives you an idea of what will be covered and imprints the main themes.

2. *Questions*   You next think up a few questions that you hope will be answered when you read it through properly.

3. *Read*   You then read it all quickly, not stopping to follow detailed arguments in all their intricacies.

4. *Recall (or recite)*   This means you close the book and trying to think of the main points, perhaps jotting them down on a piece of paper. These can form the basis of your notes if they are good enough.

5. *Review*   The last stage consists of going through the text more slowly and making your notes, adding to those from the *recall* stage or making new ones if necessary.

This approach may seem slow and cumbersome but it sure makes most people remember what they read! It is a good idea to try this SQ3R method for a few weeks to see if it works for you and if so, stick with it. Note that it is important not to try out a new system once, decide that it is too time consuming and tedious, and then give up on it. All new systems take a little getting used to.

Reading through before starting to take your notes
You should always read through the material before starting to take notes, otherwise you might end up noting the less important points or even copying the whole thing out.

Speed reading
Reading is like driving; most can do it, but few do it well. Most children are taught to read (*literacy*) but few are taught to read properly (*efficiency*). Unless you have attended special courses, you should assume you do not read as well as you might. Speed reading is actually a misnomer: it can teach you to read more quickly, but it also allows you to remember more of what you read. It teaches you to read different things at different speeds, *ie* efficiently, thereby saving you time. If your university offers a free course, it is worth doing but many commercial courses seem overpriced. Speed reading programs are now available on computers and provide a decent and cheaper alternative, as long as you persist and practise.

Some tips on reading more quickly
- When you pick up anything to read, ask yourself at what speed you should read – flat out, medium paced, or slowly.

- The first time you start to read a journal article, read only the first sentence of each paragraph then jump to the next paragraph; return to the start and read properly.

- Alternatively, read the first and last sentences of each paragraph.

- Use SQ3R if you can.

- With a newspaper or magazine, run your eye down the middle of the column, trying to understand the content.

- Try to read in small chunks, of a few words or phrases, and do not look at each word as a separate item.

MAKING USE OF RESOURCES

Learning to use the library
There has been recent rapid technological change in libraries and computers are now widely used. You need new skills to use the catalogue and other information sources, but it is easier to find material than it once was. You should go to any course that your university holds on library use, pick up any pamphlets they have, and never be afraid to ask for help. Few new students can use a university library well and the sooner you gain the skill, the better.

In the first week of term, look up the call numbers for the textbooks in your course (these are the numbers printed on the spine of the book) and go and see where they are located so you can find them again easily.

If you are searching the catalogue for material and the computer crashes you can check the printed card catalogue that many libraries still keep. It is better than fuming and wasting time.

Finding the special library sections
Markers get so bored reading virtually identical answers to a question that if you can get in something different but relevant, they are so pleased they tend to be more generous with marks. Newer data, a different diagram or a fresh example can make your assignment stand out and help you gain marks. Where can you look?

The reference section
This is a collection of basic information that is often overlooked. It is worth browsing the shelves for an hour in the first week to see what

your library holds. Make a note of the title and call number of anything that looks interesting and relevant to your course. You can use these items later for researching essays, *etc.*

Electronic databases and search tools
Ask what electronic databases (other than the catalogue) are available and what is on CD-Rom that you can use. Some newspaper, magazine and journal articles are now being put on such discs. They can be a great source of recent information, but you often have to book in advance to use them.

You need to search under a variety of words and it saves time if you think up a list in advance. For instance, if you wish to know about vegetation growth, you might think up 'vegetation, trees, shrubs, hedges, bushes, plants, grass, ground-cover, weed, weeding; soil, fertiliser, chemical fertiliser, manure, insecticides, pesticides; water, irrigation, climate, and temperature'. Note that some programs insist you check the singular as well as the plural, *eg* 'tree' and 'trees'.

The government documents section
This is where government documents, including foreign government and United Nations material will be stored. Often ignored by first-year students, it can provide useful and original information that helps your work to stand out.

Some university library tips

– Do not write in library books or add new comments to existing ones however tempting.

– Remember to keep quiet and let others study in peace.

– Do not hide books in obscure places for your own use.

– Do not forget there are other libraries in your city to try if you are desperate.

Collecting clippings of articles
You would find it interesting and useful to buy a magazine in your discipline area. Once you have paid for it, clipping articles of interest costs you nothing. Remember to put the source, including the date and page number on. If you buy a good newspaper it can be a good source

too. You can keep the clippings in old envelopes or manilla folders, filed by topic, and stored in a cardboard box. Any supermarket will be happy to give you one and you can take a folder with you to choose the best size. When you prepare an assignment the material you have collected will give you different information, personalise your answer and help gain you extra marks.

Trying the Internet for extra information
Your university may give you free access to the Internet, if not forget it unless you are seriously wealthy as timed local calls in the UK mean the phone bills can be horrendous. Free local calls in the USA and untimed local calls in Australia give those countries a real edge.

Sources of useful information
- News groups – around 14,000 in 1995 and still growing – where people swap ideas and information (may be scurrilous and rude).

- Libraries and documents (but sometimes you have to pay to get a copy).

- Programs to run (word processors, spread sheets, games . . .).

How to find the information you need
A good way to start is to go to sites of gathered references, like **Yahoo**, **Yanoff**, **Lycos**, or **Alta Vista**. You can also search on your own using different search tools, like **Archie** (good), **Gopher** (uses menus), **Veronica** (searches Gopher menus for you), **WAIS** (good for documents), or **NetCrawler**. The Internet is in a state of flux, everything keeps altering, home pages and news groups move, and new sites come on as old ones disappear. You should check any recent Internet magazine for a list of what looks useful and their current addresses. Meanwhile try http://www.open.ac.uk/ for Open University information or Yahoo on http://www.yahoo.com

The value of the Internet
It is great fun, but it can be a tremendous drain on valuable time. You should think in terms of spending hours not minutes. Currently the information you find is often poor and news groups are the haunt of the interested but ignorant, so that you get only a few gold nuggets in return for a lot of digging. Other than sheer enjoyment, the main benefit of using the Net is you will develop skills that can help when seeking a job and developing your career.

CASE STUDIES

Alan's motivation reaps results

Alan is determined to succeed and sees his future in banking or perhaps insurance. His drive has led him to set up a study group that meets regularly every other day. He dominates it a bit but it helps both him and them. He is also enjoying university and tells his spouse what he did during the day – she is a bit bored with this but puts up with it so far.

Jane finds a study-buddy

Jane was worried that she was not learning much in tutorials and talked to the university adviser who suggested she find a study-buddy, which she has now done. She is not yet confident enough to join a group. She learns a lot studying on her own but finds discussing with her buddy reinforces her knowledge and occasionally a new idea startles her. She is enjoying university life more, is starting to build up her confidence and is learning well.

Bob finds going it alone can be tough

Bob never thinks about a study-buddy or group learning and just turns up for most, but not all, of the formal sessions. He is learning a bit but not much; but he is having a really good time. He is a border line failure case and is becoming aware of it, but he vaguely hopes somehow he will manage to do better.

DISCUSSION POINTS

1. How many ways of using short periods of study time (up to half an hour) can you think of for your particular course or subjects?

2. What sort of learning game can you invent for an informal study group?

3. Where exactly can you find practise questions for the subjects you are studying?

SUMMARY

- Go over your notes regularly, preferably each day.
- Explaining your notes to another is an excellent way of learning.
- Condensing your notes is valuable.
- Take advantage of short periods of time and do not waste them.

- Practise planning a skeleton answer to a few questions each day.

- Pay more attention to the comments on your essays than the mark you get.

- A study-buddy will help you learn more quickly and make it fun.

- A study group allows you to play various games that will improve your performance.

- You must buy the set textbooks and should use it wisely.

- Try to read different types of material at different speeds.

- The SQ3R approach helps: Survey – Question – Read – Recall – Review.

- Learn how to use your library's computerised databases.

- Keep your own clippings and use them for extra marks.

- So far, the Internet can take up a lot of time for relatively little return.

4
Using Formal Teaching Sessions

You should go to all the set teaching sessions and not be tempted to miss any. Once you start missing things, it gets harder to build your knowledge on the increasingly shaky framework. Your motivation to study and succeed will also start to evaporate. Only if you find some lecturer is truly hopeless, would you be better off skipping his or her lectures. If you make this decision, make sure you study in that time period.

MAKING THE MOST OF LECTURES

The teaching methods at university are often different from those you had at school and you may have to learn a few new tricks.

Using the syllabus and outlines provided

Many lecturers provide course outlines, including lecture schedules containing recommended reading. If your lecturer does not do this, a note asking if they would do so, with a little flattery about helping you to follow the excellent lectures, might pay off. Once you have a course handout, read it over regularly and get the 'shape' of the course in your mind. Whenever a new topic is begun in the lectures, check the handout to see how far you have got and how it fits in. Doing this helps to increase your motivation to study and also makes learning easier. Some lecturers provide an outline of each lecture; if your lecturer does this, use it to clarify the organisation of the lecture but still take notes or annotate the outline – it will be insufficient on its own. As the course proceeds, if you get extra handouts containing information drawn from the lectures this is prime information that you are expected to know. Read such handouts regularly and memorise them.

Psyching yourself up before the lecture

If your course handout tells you what part of the textbook to read for each lecture, make sure you do this before the lecture is given. It will help you to follow the lecture as well as understand and remember the content more easily. Before the lecture you can also review this material with your study-buddy and tell each other what the textbook meant; this is a very effective way of learning. It will also reveal any weak points in your understanding and may provoke questions, which you can ask in the lecture hall, if this is allowed.

On the way to the lecture hall, it will help you if you go over in your mind what was in the assigned reading and consider which bits the lecturer might focus on. This mental tuning up will make your learning easier.

Getting there early

Choose to sit in a place in which you feel comfortable and where you can easily hear the lecture and see the board. Many students sit in roughly the same place each week as it makes them feel relaxed and comfortable. Once you are settled, psych yourself up if you did not do this on the way to the lecture hall. You should try to feel positive about how interesting the lecture will be, and ask yourself things like: will it follow the textbook, will it contradict it, or will the questions you thought up be answered? You should try to put out of your mind any feelings of boredom or dislike. You can also use the time to read over last week's lecture notes.

Avoiding wasting your time in the lecture hall

If you are going to sit there for an hour, you might as well get the most out of it. Sitting and daydreaming in a university lecture is a total waste of your time. Also, once the lecture starts you should avoid chatting with the people around you. If you want to discuss last night's TV show, go outside and do it. No one forces you to be at the lecture, it is merely in your interest to be there and pay attention. Also avoid giggling with friends, which disrupts the lecture and prevents other students from concentrating.

If you find your attention wandering in lectures, try to bring your mind back; perhaps you could think briefly about the job you want after you graduate (in order to raise the level of your motivation), or look over the lecture outline if you have one, then settle down to concentrating again. Do not be overly concerned if this mind-wandering happens to you now and then, but do fight it.

Taking good lecture notes

What do you need?

You will need to buy a cheap lined pad (a margin is useful for your comments) and A4 is the best size. A ring folder is essential. You might also find a clipboard handy if you have to stand up to take notes. You will need one or two different coloured pens, or a multicoloured one. Really cheap ballpoint pens tend to blob and smear and it is worth paying a little extra to get a better one. A transparent plastic ruler can be handy, but only a few specific courses need a set square. You might find a pencil useful for copying diagrams – if you make a mistake it is easily rectified using an eraser. You can ink it in later.

Start slowly and only buy things when you really need them. Ultimately you might find you need a stapler, paper clips, white-out, several different coloured pens, some overhead transparencies, special overhead transparency pens in perhaps three different colours, scissors, adhesive tape, maybe a hole punch, and a cheap calculator.

How you should take notes

At the top you should put the lecture topic, date, and lecturer's name – it can be useful later on to know where you got the information. You should write on one side of the page only if you can afford it because it makes it much easier to find things later. When your notes are in your ring folder, it means you have a blank left-hand page for your comments, ideas and any additions you might want to make and it is easier to slot new notes in the proper place.

Listening for what's important

The lecture will have a skeleton framework in logical order that has been padded out into words. Your task is to extract that framework and the main points within it; do not write down everything that is said, especially jokes and asides. Try to listen rather than write down everything and make sure you note the main points, any criticisms of the textbook or a particular person's views, and all diagrams, figures, tables, and references supplied.

Note-taking techniques

Using the dot-dash method of note-taking can be handy. The main headings get a dot in front of them, subheads are inset about a centimetre with a dash in front of the first word, sub-subheads are inset, again with a dot, and so on. You might wish to replace the dots and dashes with numbers later, if seeing them will help you to remember your notes.

Making your notes clear

It is tempting but wrong to save money by squashing up your writing – try not to be stingy with paper and leave plenty of room for your comments. A wide margin is useful for this and some students draw in a right-hand margin for that purpose. If you make your notes a

≠	not equals
∴	therefore
<	less than
=	equals
>	more than
asap	as soon as possible
cf.	compared with
comm.	communication
eg	for example
fig.	figure
ibid.	in the same passage or book (footnotes)
ie	that is
inc.	including; incorporated
k	kilogram, kilometre
L	necessarily (logical symbol)
loc. cit.	at the place quoted (footnotes)
M	possibly (logical symbol)
op. cit	in the work cited (footnotes)
PC	personal computer, politically correct, police constable
PM	Prime Minister

Fig. 3. Some examples of useful standard abbreviations.

pleasure to look at and not all cramped up, you will read them more often and learn the content more easily. Lay out your notes logically in clear handwriting, using one or two different colours if you wish. It is easier to go through them after the lecture and underline headings and important points in different colours rather than at the time. The use of colour helps the important things to stand out and makes visual recall easier. If you read your notes often enough, you can get to picture them in your mind.

When taking notes you should always use abbreviations where you can. Many reasonably standard ones exist – Figure 3 provides examples of some of these.

You can and should invent your own abbreviations suitable for your course which will make note-taking easier. You can use symbols, for example:

↑	Increase
↓	Decrease
→	Causes; leads to
~	Not
Σ	Everything; the total

Dealing with problems that emerge in the lecture

You are likely to have an occasional problem of not understanding something in a lecture – what can you do?

1. Some universities allow questions – raise your hand, and cough if you are not noticed.

2. Some lecturers deliberately leave time for questions at the end.

3. Some will stay back to answer questions after the hour is up.

4. You can go and ask the lecturer about it during office hours (take your notes with you with the place marked so you can find it easily).

5. Look up the textbook to see if the point is covered there.

6. Look the point up in a few different textbooks.

7. Ask another tutor or lecturer about it.

8. Listen to the tape of the lecture you or your university made.

9. Discuss the question with your study-buddy or study group.

If the problem is that the lecturer goes too quickly and covers too much, it is probably because they have no choice in the matter and have a set syllabus to get through in a fixed time. Discussing with your study-buddy will often let you catch up and fill in bits you may have missed.

Taping the lectures
Some universities tape the first-year lectures and put them in the library. Check to see if yours does this. If not, you might find it useful to tape the lecture yourself. If you do this, it is polite to ask permission of the lecturer in the theatre the first time you do it. After that a smile will usually suffice as you put the machine down.

The benefits of taping lectures
If you missed a bit of the lecture, maybe you came in late or lost concentration briefly, you can check the tape to see what was said. If you miss a lecture and use a tape to catch up, you should always listen to the whole tape before you start taking notes. This helps you to sort out the logical framework and also to remember what was said because you hear it twice.

The limitations of taping lectures
Taping is not a substitute for attending a lecture because many lecturers write important concepts of the lecture on the board as they talk and you miss this. In addition, you cannot see any diagrams, maps, *etc* that the lecturer may indicate and the tape can be fuzzy and indistinct with missing bits. Taping the lecture yourself may carry the danger that the tape runs out before the end.

Going over the lecture material afterwards
It will help you to remember the information if you go over your notes relatively shortly after the lecture; certainly the same day. Apart from this early reinforcement, you can add the colours, underlines, and margin comments to your notes at the same time. It is valuable to compare your lecture notes with your study-buddy or group, to discuss the issues and explain points to each other. You might find you missed

something important and it should make a lot more sense after the discussion. A further glance over your notes the next day and you should be well on the way to remembering the information.

Wasting time copying them out
It is generally useless to laboriously copy out lecture notes again. It is of little value in helping you to remember them, and it is a better use of your time to reread them, and then discuss with others or explain the issues and concepts involved.

MAKING THE MOST OF TUTORIALS AND SEMINARS

Preparing well beforehand
You need to do some work before you go to a tutorial or seminar: just turning up and hoping to get something out of the session is like going into a battle unarmed. You should read whatever material was set and make a few notes about it, including any criticisms you have and an indication of what you think. After that, it would help you to spend half an hour discussing it with your study-buddy. If nothing was set, try looking up the general issue in a textbook in advance.

At the tutorial or seminar
In the session, you will listen to a paper, take a few notes, and ask questions at the end. The reading you did earlier, plus whatever you gleaned from the paper, should be enough to allow you to think up a question or two. If you ask the first (sensible) question it gets you noticed and you start to build up a reputation for ability.

Taking notes in tutorials and seminars
If the topic is new to you, you might wish to extract the paper's outline and main points, but if you already know something about the subject, just the new and interesting points and sources might be enough.

Participating and joining in
Do not sit like a pudding and let the discussion flow around, but try to ask questions and join in. You will learn more about the subject and clarify your own ideas and position, as well as learning how to defend a view and, if necessary, to change your mind gracefully. This is a good place to learn such skills, as there is no penalty if your idea is erroneous or only partially true, unlike in the exam room.

Attending tutorials and seminars
You should always go to the tutorials and seminars, even if the title

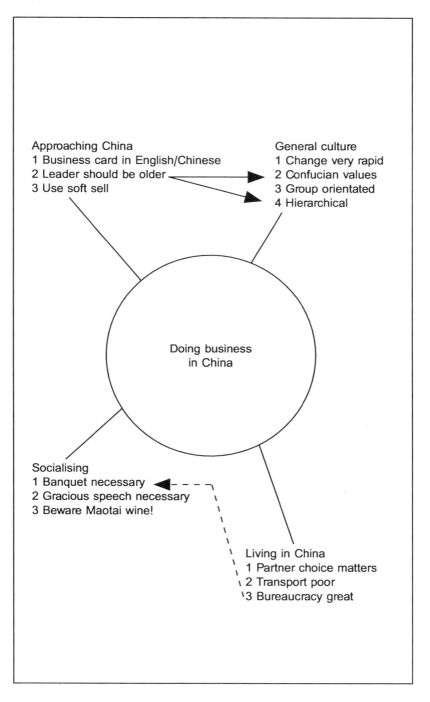

Fig. 4. The pattern method of note-taking.

sounds boring. It may be better than you expect and in any case it will be assumed that henceforth you will understand the issue. Even if it doesn't seem relevant immediately, the information you get may be needed later in the course, and you gain skills from the process.

Presenting a paper

When you have to give a paper, choosing to go early in the term is best. Although presenting in the first few weeks sounds alarming, the marker may be more lenient because s/he knows you've had little time to prepare. You also get one assignment out of the way and can then relax a bit. A further reason is that if you should fall ill and have to postpone delivering a paper, it is easier to reschedule if it was early on. Apart from that, towards the end of the term, the exams are looming, long essays may be due, and you will start to feel short of time. If it is possible, you should try to scatter your assignments over the first three quarters of the term and leave the last two or three weeks free for revision or any catching up sessions you have to do.

MAKING THE MOST OF WORKSHOPS AND LABS

Prepare in advance

There will probably be preliminary set readings or exercises to do, depending on the nature of your subject. It is important you do these in advance so that you get the most out of the sessions.

In the workshop or lab

In workshops you need to get in and do things, participating as much as you can. You should avoid sitting back and coasting which does not develop any of the skills you need. The more you participate – entering into the debate, discussing alternatives, arguing against the set material or the views of others – the more you benefit. However, it is best not to present a silly view and argue it strongly just for effect, because this will annoy your fellow students.

Note-taking in group work

As well as discussing, arguing, and using equipment all the time, you should take notes about what was done and said, or observations you made, as well as any tutor's comments.

The pattern method

This is a free form method of note-taking which can be particularly effective when you are in a free-ranging discussion that can jump about a lot. Figure 4 gives an example of the pattern method.

If you spread out the headings and leave plenty of space you can return to any particular bit of the issue and add any extra points as they emerge. You can also easily show interlinks between the points, one way or two way.

CASE STUDIES

Alan participates well

Alan participates strongly in tutorials and workshops and is beginning to be regarded as a leading light. He is so enthusiastic, the tutor has already had to restrain him to let the others have a turn, but he took this well. He really enjoys the workshops and looks forward to them. He gets a reasonable amount from lectures but he is not yet adept at extracting the main framework and is dimly aware that he could do better here.

Jane gains most from lectures

Jane gets lots from lectures and psychs herself up by going over last week's notes, doing the set reading and thinking about it. Her only weakness is she has a tendency to write down everything the lecturer says. She gets less from tutorials, and less again from workshops, where she is too shy to say anything and only sits and listens. She learns a bit from the general discussion but far less than she could if she joined in. She understands she needs to loosen up but finds it hard because she is shy. She is plucking up the courage to see the university adviser and talk about what she can do about it.

Bob is gaining little from lectures

Bob just turns up to lectures without any psyching up period so he is getting less from them than he should. He gets distracted easily and if he thinks of something he tends to chat with one of his friends, missing part of the lecture. Although he does not prepare in advance, he gets quite a bit from the workshops, as he participates strongly – really because he enjoys talking with friends. Already he has missed a couple of lectures and a tutorial and feels he is no worse off – wrongly!

DISCUSSION POINTS

1. What could you do to make where you sit in the lecture hall a better place to learn in?

2. Do you enjoy questioning and arguing? If not, what could you do to help you to join in tutorial discussions?

3. How many ways can you think of for reviewing your notes after lectures and tutorials? Can you invent a game for two or more people to do this together?

SUMMARY

- You should go to all the set lectures, tutorials, *etc.*

- Get hold of a syllabus or course outline and study it.

- Psych yourself up before each lecture, tutorial or workshop.

- Do not waste your time when in lectures, *etc.*

- Take good notes in formal sessions, especially in lectures.

- Do not rely solely on taped lectures.

- Go over your lecture notes the same day for early reinforcement.

- Prepare in advance for tutorials and workshops.

- Join in the discussion in tutorials and workshops.

- Do your tutorial paper early if you can.

5
Organising Information and Preparing Answers

When you study at university you will find your notes continually expand but they don't come in any logical order. It will make your life easier if you organise your notes so that you can quickly find what you want. This will help you when you come to prepare assignments.

FILING YOUR NOTES FOR EASY ACCESS

Your daily file
Each day you will make notes at the university and these are most easily and safely carried in a ring binder or envelope file. Put your name and department on it, so that if you lose it someone might hand it in. A set of file dividers with a tab for each subject keeps them orderly in a ring binder.

Your permanent files
Ring binders are fine for your stock of notes at home. Use one for each subject and separate the notes into sections with dividers. Box files could be used instead but they are harder to organise internally. Envelope files or manilla folders are cheap and work well. You do not need to buy a filing cabinet, as you can store your files in a cardboard box. Using a different coloured folder for different courses helps keep things organised. Before you reach for the white-out, note that you can re-use old manilla folders with names on if you turn them back to front or inside out.

Putting notes on a computer
Normally it is not worth putting your notes on a computer or typing them up as it takes time that could be better spent learning them. There is one exception to this: if your writing is truly awful, you might wish to put your notes on a computer for printing up, or retrieving later but there is little learning function in doing this. If you are rich and have a scanner, you can put notes into a computer relatively easily, but they are not perfect and you still have to go through making corrections. For most students, a computer is best used for preparing and writing assignments

not keeping notes. If you must put them on you have a choice of a word processor or a database. Word processors are easier to use and you will develop computer skills necessary for writing. You can also copy from the notes and paste them into an essay easily. A database is initially a bit harder to use, and you develop a different set of skills.

STARTING THE ASSIGNMENT

Every assignment you do goes through three stages:

- you gather information and organise it
- you read your notes, decide what you think, and plan your answer
- you write it up.

For good marks at university, the first two stages are the really important ones, although paradoxically many students tend to worry more about the writing stage. When you get the first two stages right, the essay almost writes itself.

Discussing the issue with others can also provide valuable assistance in preparing an assignment and can help you gain even better marks. Figure 5 illustrates the stages of preparing an assignment.

Making a start

If you have an urgent assignment to prepare and you have been putting it off – start now! Pick up a pen and a piece of paper and start jotting down things like:

- what you think about the topic
- why you think you were afraid to begin
- any ideas on how it might be organised
- where you might find information about it
- any famous names that are associated with the topic
- who you know that you could talk to about it
- a rough skeleton for a possible answer.

Improving your mental attitude

Lay aside the list of ideas you have just made, then return to it in about 20 minutes. Look it over, tell yourself the question is interesting, and persuade yourself that you look forward to finding out as much about it as you can. Maybe picking up a book on the issue and reading the contents page will be all you need to get you interested. You can try talking to your study-buddy or group about the topic. You should find your interest develops with such activity and some thought.

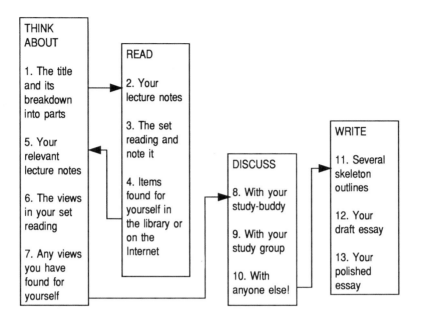

Fig. 5. How to prepare an assignment.

Deciding how you will present your oral

You can write an essay and read it out: this is easier, safer and usually best in your first year. Alternatively, you can present the oral purely from notes: this is harder but develops your confidence, capacity to persuade, and skills in public speaking. It is worth trying in later years (see Chapter 10 for ways of doing this).

Dividing major tasks into manageable parts

It is easy to feel too afraid to begin if the question seems big and difficult – it isn't really! Big topics need not frighten you. All you have to do is to divide it into manageable sections or bites and keep nibbling away at it until it is done. Start with a simple skeleton outline and keep expanding it by dividing more and more finely. The big project should then seem easier when each separate part of your plan looks feasible.

Gathering the information

When you have begun thinking about the assignment in this way, what do you do next? It is always best to start with the easy and big, then move later to the more difficult and small. Follow these suggested stages:

1. Start with your textbook.

2. Then use your lecture notes.

3. Then go to your notes from tutorials, seminars, workshops, *etc.*

4. Then go to the library – don't forget the encyclopaedias and 'Dictionaries of...' relevant to your discipline – these are good places to start.

5. Look up your lecturer's name in case they have published in that area and at least list them in the bibliography if they have.

6. Then move on to other specialist library books via the catalogue.

7. Then see whether the journals contain anything useful for your topic.

8. You might try the CD-Roms in the library.

9. Finally, use your own files of clippings to personalise your answer for a better mark.

DETERMINING THE BEST WAY TO TACKLE THE QUESTION

What might go in

The approach of WWWWWH
The 'WWWWWH' approach (one 'W' for one hand's fingers and thumb) is taught to cadet journalists and stands for **what, who, when, where, why, and how.** Designed for newspaper purposes, it is not usually totally appropriate for university assignments, but it may help you not to miss out something valuable.

Other questions you might ask yourself
• What are the causes and effects?
• What is the relative importance of each issue?
• Does it clash with other theories or data I have and how can I explain that?
• What do I personally think about it?

Important ingredients in an assignment
- an introduction, main body of text, and a conclusion
- a logical organisation
- the introduction consistent with your conclusion
- analysing, not merely describing
- maintaining a theme (if this is appropriate to the question).

Some recommended approaches
1. Try putting one idea in one paragraph.
2. Try presenting the standard case before going on to criticisms of it.

Recognising standard forms of questions
Some questions may seem complex or obscure initially but generally they will all be asking you to do one of the following:

1. To give the case for something, the case against, and summing up (analyse and provide judgement).

2. To compare and contrast two different theories or events.

3. To estimate the effects of A on B (judging the importance of links).

4. To estimate how much A...N caused X (judging the relative importance).

5. To comment on a statement or quotation (often involves links and judging the importance).

6. To explain some facts or work out what will happen from a given situation (often means applying a model).

In almost every case the marker is looking for you to display some factual knowledge, an ability to organise and to reason, and then to reach a considered judgement based on the evidence you have presented. The following are some examples of approaches to questions which don't do this and therefore often lead to poor marks:

- describing what happened without analysing it
- using a straight chronological approach
- not answering the question that was asked, but drifting into a different one
- not using a theoretical model when one or more are available.

Organising the information

Two particularly useful approaches when organising information for projects are **SWOT** and **SMEAC**.

What is SWOT?

SWOT is an acronym describing an approach which can be useful for analysing and writing up a project. It stands for:

- **strengths** of the project
- **weaknesses** of the project
- **opportunities** that exist or could be created
- **threats** from competing firms, countries or groups.

What is SMEAC?

SMEAC is an acronym that stands for:

- **situation**, or what we are looking at
- **mission**: the business objectives or goals of the people involved
- **execution** of the project, including the stages of reaching the goals
- **administration**: who plans it; who runs it; who funds it and how
- **communication** with interested parties.

Who the interested parties are depends entirely on the particular project, but the category often includes areas like marketing and advertising; product distribution; various government and other regulatory bodies (existing relationships and the need to build new ones); and business partners (existing and new ones).

DECIDING WHAT YOU THINK

Some points to be aware of

1. Some of what you have been told and believe to be true is in fact untrue, or only partially true, but you do not know which bits. When someone disagrees with you, keep an open mind, they just might be right.

2. What you think of as normal or reasonable behaviour may not be what others will do.

3. You cannot rely on your own experience to determine what is the truth. A sample of one is always too small.

4. Plausibility does mean a thing is true.

5. Consistency does not prove an argument is true.

6. Repetition does not mean truth.

7. A larger number of supporters does not mean truth.

8. The views of someone you like or trust need not be true.

9. The latest information is not necessarily true.

10. The degree of complexity of an argument bears no necessary relationship with the truth.

11. Truth is best revealed by testing theories against the facts. As new theories and facts emerge, what we believe to be true gets refined and alters.

12. Different people can accept the same model (or version of the truth) but still have different opinions if their priorities or values differ.

Sketching out a preliminary approach
Start with a pen and paper and put down what immediately jumps into mind. The pattern method of note-taking which was discussed on page 62, allows you to organise your early ideas nicely, so you might try it first. The skeleton approach is more logical and might be used next, because it helps you to get your ideas in a suitable order for writing.

Discussing the topic with others
Your study-buddy and study group are your best option for discussions. If you have avoided developing either, then you will have to make use of any close friend. **Brainstorming** the topic is valuable at any stage before you write, as it helps you to organise your thoughts and exposes any weak points.

Assessing data reliability
Sometimes you will find conflicting views and evidence. What can you do to help choose between them?

1. Ask yourself if the author has an axe to grind (political; nationalist; religion; race ...).

2. Consider the author's likely ability (have you heard of him/her; who does s/he work for?).

3. Who published the book or journal? (are they respectable; are they well known?).

If no other considerations are involved you might prefer:

- UN data over national sources
- national data over one institute's data
- official statistics over private
- statements by well-known authorities in the area
- a work coming from a major publisher
- journals over magazines and especially over newspapers
- later data rather than earlier.

Note: statements from such sources are not necessarily better; but pragmatically they are easier for you to justify using.

CHOOSING WHAT TO LEAVE OUT

When you have gathered sufficient information, you may have to decide what to discard. This is the penalty of knowing a lot. One guide is to keep asking yourself if the particular point or piece of data is strictly relevant. You can do this by regularly going back to check the title and your skeleton outline.

Choosing your own approach
Except in a few areas of maths, there is no such thing as the *correct* answer, only a choice of approaches. You often have to **devise your own approach** and determine what boundaries you will put on the topic, drawing your own lines. In this, you must be sensible and always be prepared to defend the boundary lines and your approach. As a handy rule of thumb, it almost always pays to address a question from a theoretical point of view, using a model if appropriate. You can then present data and examples to justify what you are saying.

Monitoring the length of the paper

How long should it be?
This question is asked every year by students. If you have not been given a maximum number of words or guide to length then the real answer is *as long as it needs*, which isn't a lot of help. You should ask your tutor or lecturer what sort of length is expected or check with last year's students. As a very rough guide, for essays in many subjects, papers in the first year might be four to eight typed pages long, when

double spaced. A term paper will be longer than a weekly one of course. Rarely is one A4 page enough except perhaps in a subject like maths. With oral papers, around 20 minutes might suffice.

Anticipating possible oral questions
Knowing the sort of questions you may be asked can reduce your nervousness and allow you to perform better.

The main types of questions
- *Factual*: 'Did you say earlier that …?'; 'Did you find that …?'; 'Did you consult …?'

- *Expressing a view and asking for a comment*: 'I think that … I would value your comments'. This one often opens up the discussion more widely.

- *Pointing out a weakness or missing elements*: 'Possibly you underrated the influence of …' or 'I saw no mention of …' Be prepared to explain why you feel it is less significant.

- *Pointing to implications*: 'What you said about X, suggests that…' This often involves asking how it fits in with other events or conflicting theories or interpretations.

Making handouts
For oral presentations, in some courses it is stipulated that you must give a handout to each student present. Even if not forced to do so, it is still a good idea, as it will impress the staff member and can gain you marks.

What could go on your handout?
- your name and the topic title, together with the course and date
- the outline of your talk
- any data or diagrams you will use.

Handout tips
- Use both sides of the paper when you are photocopying to save money.
- Make sure there are no silly spelling errors or other mistakes.
- Do not make your handout an exact replica of an overhead transparency (OHT).
- A long handout can cause people to look down reading and prevent you gaining eye contact.

Avoiding plagiarism

Plagiarism is copying someone else's work and presenting it as your own. It is a deadly sin at university, it is embarrassing if you are discovered, and it is severely punished. If you are found out, a careful eye will be kept on you in future, your reputation will suffer and you will find it harder to get a decent reference when seeking that first job. It also means you fail to develop useful skills and are unlikely to remember what you copied.

CASE STUDIES

Alan doesn't prepare thoroughly enough

Alan starts to prepare his first assignment but his enthusiasm causes him to skip ahead and he starts to write too early, relying on his ability to get him through. He buys a good newspaper but does not clip it and has not investigated the library's CD-Roms. He cannot expect a great mark but does not yet realise this.

Jane's good preparation leads to good marks

Jane prepares well. She invents several different skeleton answers and keeps adjusting the latest one as she finds more information – she uses the CD-Rom databases in the library and her own clippings for extra information, and has found a very useful UN survey of the field in the government section of the library.

Bob pays the penalties of poor preparation

Bob does little preparation and has not yet found his way around the library. He starts by writing down a few ideas but he doesn't develop a proper skeleton outline, and his poor mark reflects this. He never buys a newspaper or any magazines and spends his spare time and money in the bar. He will later find it difficult to write because he doesn't actually know what he wants to say.

DISCUSSION POINTS

1. Which do you think is the more important, planning the outline of an assignment or writing it up?

2. Where would you start looking for information about an assignment in your subject? Where might you find relevant information in a place few might think of looking in your library?

3. If you have a major assignment to do and have been putting it off,

what could you do to force yourself to start?

SUMMARY

- File your notes by topic and in a way that lets you find them when needed.
- Never be afraid to start working on an assignment.
- Tutorial papers are usually better written out, then read aloud.
- Consider carefully how best to tackle the question.
- The SWOT and SMEAC approaches can be useful.
- You may have to decide between sources of different reliability.
- Design your own approach, draw your boundary lines, and be prepared to defend both.
- Try to guess what questions you might be asked in your tutorial.
- Prepare a handout when you are giving a tutorial.
- Copying other people's work does not help you to develop.

6
Giving an Oral Paper

For many people, the first time they have to deliver an oral paper is at university and it can be a bit frightening. What is the best way to tackle it? (It is assumed that you will read aloud from a written script. If you choose to present it from notes instead, see Chapter 10.)

DOING A DRY RUN

You should hold a practice session the day before and read your paper aloud: this rehearsal allows you to see how long it takes and will help build your confidence. Read it out loud slowly at the speed you will adopt in the session. If your paper is too long or too short you can perhaps adjust it, but note that generally more papers tend to be too long. Ask your study-buddy or a friend to listen, time it and watch you, and then to give helpful critical comments about your voice and body language as well as the content.

COPING WITH NERVES

Learning to relax
Feeling nervous is normal and useful – you can use it to improve your motivation. Excessive fear, however, is not helpful, especially if you blank out temporarily and forget what you have learned. It is valuable to learn how to relax, not only for oral presentations but also before exams or interviews and in times of personal stress. It can even help you to fall asleep at night. There are a number of different ways of relaxing and you might already be adept at one. If not, some techniques are presented here for you to try.

Note: you should never simply take lots of deep breaths to try to relax as it can be dangerous and cause you to hyperventilate.

Determining which relaxation technique to use
Try each of the following techniques – one a day – to see which one works best for you. Start by taking your pulse and make a note of the

rate. Then try one technique for maybe half an hour, and afterwards take your pulse again. Write it down and compare the two results and you will see how much that technique slowed your heart beat down. After a few days you can compare all the results and see which technique slows your heart down the most – this is the most effective one for you. Practise your chosen method for a few weeks and you will get even better at it. Note that a full relaxation session might last for up to an hour, but even a few minutes are beneficial. If at first you find you have a tendency to smile or giggle, ignore it. It is a defence mechanism – your subconscious mind may worry about this new event and try to reject it. Once it accepts the process as beneficial, the tendency to giggle should disappear.

Relaxation technique one: imagining a rural scene
You lie quietly on your back, arms by your side, palms up or down and with your fingers relaxed and slightly curled. Keep your eyes closed and consciously try to relax for ten seconds. If you are unable to lie down, you can sit in a comfortable chair with your arms on your thighs. You now picture a peaceful rural scene (you drifting in a boat on a lake, sauntering down a country lane, sitting in a glade in a wood ...) with all its sounds. Hold and enjoy the calm, quiet picture.

Relaxation technique two: tackling the offending muscles
You lie, sit, *etc* as above. Take your attention to your jaw and mouth and consciously slacken the muscles, letting your jaw sag. Do the same with your neck and shoulders, then fingers and toes. Continue going round the rest of your body for best results, then relax and enjoy. A variation of the technique is first to tighten up a muscle group and hold it tense for five to ten seconds then let go suddenly, before moving on to the next set of muscles.

Relaxation technique three: the simple breath approach
You lie, sit, *etc* as above. Then try one of the following ways of varying this technique.

Variation A – Take your attention to your toes and breathe in slowly, picturing and feeling your breath flowing over your feet, up your legs and over the top of your body to your head; as you breathe out, picture and feel your breath running down your back all the way to your heels. Keep it up for as long as you like – maybe one or two minutes if in an exam room and short of time or up to 30 minutes or so if at home.

Variation B – Picture the whole world around you as gleaming silvery white; as you breathe in slowly the breath is bright and silvery; as you breathe out it is dark and gloomy as you expel toxins. Timing as for A.

Variation C – If you can identify any particular plain, discomfort or weakness in any area of your body, imagine that the silvery breath is going into it and healing it or driving it away.

Relaxation technique four: the count down
You lie, sit, *etc* as above. Choose a number – try 10 to 20 if under pressure in the exam room, 100 if at home. Each breath will count for one. Starting with 20 as an example, breathe in slowly, thinking of the number and visualising it in your head, and breathe out. Then change to 19, visualising yourself moving down to it, and breathe in and out. Continue counting down to zero and stop, and just enjoy the relaxed feeling of *being*. If you forget what number you are on it doesn't matter – just relax and go back to the last number you can remember. When you've had enough, count your breaths up from one to five, one breath at a time, before opening your eyes.

Quick relaxation: facial massage
Sit quietly, close your eyes and relax. Then using your middle and index fingers, slowly and gently rub small circles on the spot in the centre of your forehead; then move to the temples at the side of your forehead and do them together. Keep it up for a minute or two then sit quietly and enjoy the feeling. It is even better if you can persuade your partner to do it for you.

Joining a group
If you still feel ultra nervous before public speaking, you might consider **joining a group** which puts you in the public eye and lets you develop skills and confidence. The university drama group is good for this and usually has great parties! More formal are groups like Toastmasters, which train you in public speaking and give you practise. It is a strain at first if you are shy, but it gets easier and you will learn valuable skills for life.

READING THE PAPER TO YOUR BEST ADVANTAGE

Of the three elements of the paper: content, organisation and presentation, you have already done the first two and only presentation is left.

Get there a little early

It will increase your tension if you are running late so try and get there early. If you are going to use any OHTs check they are in the order you will use them. When people are seated and the hour arrives, pass round your handout. With a large group, it is quicker to split the pile into two or more and send them in different directions.

Looking round the group

Try to look briefly in everybody's eyes as you do this, then introduce the topic by reading out the title: 'Today I am going to examine...'

Ignore the latecomers

There are usually a few latecomers. Ignore them completely unless they apologise to you, in which case smile and nod but do not speak to them. You should never stop to give them a handout or explain what they have missed, because this would break your flow and irritate those who came on time.

Moving from one section to another

It is good to give signposts for the listeners, so that they know where you and they are as you move from one section to another. You can do this by numbers, *eg* 'the second cause'; 'the third cause', *etc* or you can state the name of the section firmly, *eg* 'turning to the results of the action...'. It also helps if you pause slightly before you switch sections. You can glance up as you do this and get some eye contact, which helps your presentation.

Read slowly

Most people read aloud too quickly when they are nervous. Listen to yourself speaking and slow down if necessary. Remember that public speaking requires a much slower rate of delivery than normal speech.

Running over time

If you are running over time, the staff member may intervene and ask you to finish quickly. If this happens to you, smile politely and say 'two minutes', then look at your watch, and make sure you keep to that limit. You can then simply read out the headings you would have liked to cover, point out you would be happy to answer questions about those bits (a sneaky and often effective way of getting the information in later!), and then jump straight to your conclusion which you can read out.

USING GOOD BODY LANGUAGE

Poor body language can earn you lower marks if the assessor is unimpressed.

Looking out for nervous habits

When nervous, people tend to do unattractive things like:

- twisting their fingers and wringing their hands
- desperately clutching their jacket or dress
- twisting or pulling at their hair
- fiddling with buttons, ties or skirts
- touching and pulling at their ears, moustaches or eyebrows
- scratching themselves
- biting their nails.

Check yourself as you speak, or ask a close friend to observe you and report back. If you have any such bad habits, work at eliminating them. Such movements distract the listeners and reduce the impact of what you have to say. A good rule is to keep your hands away from your face and head at all times.

USING YOUR VOICE WELL

Listen to the sound of your own voice as you read aloud. Avoid slang, swear words or street jargon. If your voice is naturally high pitched or shrill:

- try to lower it consciously while delivering the paper
- practise humming a few long low notes each day for a minute or two which should gradually lower the pitch, but stop if it hurts at all; you do not wish to damage your voice.

Try to modulate and keep altering your voice when you speak by:

- consciously changing its depth and volume
- varying your speed
- trying to add warmth when it is appropriate
- keeping it interesting and try not to drone on at one level.

DEALING WITH QUESTIONS

Tell the truth – if you don't know, it's usually best to say so. Then try to find a quick analogy or something relevant to say, *eg* 'however we might feel that looking at the temperature of the reaction...'. Alternatively, you can admit lack of knowledge and immediately ask for another question and pass on quickly. If you get a difficult question you can buy time and make the questioner feel good with stalling phrases like: 'I'm glad you asked that'; 'That's a very good question'; 'That really is an interesting point' or 'That puts us into a fascinating areas...'. However, if a questioner offers an example or analogy that contradicts what you have said, you must immediately refuse to accept that analogy or you can end up in deep trouble.

CASE STUDIES

Alan enjoys his first oral presentation
With his maturity and experience in amateur dramatics, Alan looked forward to the challenge and did well. He prepared a neat and helpful handout, talked well, used lots of eye contact and was most persuasive. He received a mark of A- and is pleased with this.

Jane finds her oral a trial
Jane could not sleep well the night before and was a bundle of nerves on the day. She had prepared an excellent paper but her presentation was not good. She was nervous and it showed. She went fast and had to be asked twice to slow down. She also twisted her hair in the fingers of one hand as she read aloud in a timid voice. However, her handout was good and the actual content of the paper was even better. The tutor was sharp enough to recognise the merit of the content but was unduly influenced by her manner and she only got a mark of B, which disappointed her as she felt she had dealt with the question very well.

Bob takes it lightly
Bob did not want to present his paper and felt scared though he hid it quite well. The paper was rather lightweight, his presentation was boring and he tended to drone on. He was lucky to scrape a pass mark from a tutor who happened to feel merciful that day.

DISCUSSION POINTS

1. Do you have any nervous habits? (If you do not know, ask your friends to tell you honestly!) Have you noticed whether your friends have any?

2. Do you naturally speak quickly or slowly? Do you have a light or deep

voice? Do you say 'er' or something similar when talking? What can you do to improve your speaking and get rid of bad habits?

3. What ways of combating stress do you know about? Have you tried any? How well did it work for you?

SUMMARY

- Do a dry run first.
- Practise a relaxation technique regularly.
- Make eye contact with the audience.
- Slow your speech down and do not gabble.
- Guard against fidgeting and other nervous habits.
- Listen to yourself speaking and use your voice to good effect.

7
Writing Your Essay

Writing essays at university can be a trial for some, especially in their first year. This chapter shows you how to do it.

PREPARING TO WRITE

Writing up is simply the last stage of the assignment process. **Always be sure you know what you think and wish to say before you start to write.** 'I cannot write' often really means 'I have not read and thought enough and do not know what I really want to say'. You might find you need to prepare several different skeleton outlines before you are ready to write.

Writing up the essay
You must write an essay out properly in sentences and never use note form. Write it on a computer if you can; it is easy to move sections around, spell-check it, and print it up. At the printing stage, double space it, which looks better and encourages the marker to make more comments which are valuable. Typing is the next best way. Try not to put in handwritten assignments which look poor, and can earn you lower marks if the assessor gets fed up trying to read it. If you must write by hand, use black or dark blue ink, and leave wide margins to encourage comments. You should draw any diagrams and figures carefully using a ruler and more than one colour if they are complex. Avoid using red, because the marker may wish to use it to correct or add to the diagram.

ESSAY TIPS – THINGS TO AVOID

'Before I answer this...'
Don't begin with this phrase, it automatically causes you to answer a question that you were not asked and ensures you are sidetracked at once.

Slang and colloquial English
Slang and colloquialisms have no place in written essays, but can

sometimes be used effectively in small doses in oral presentations.

Humour
Few people have the gift of humorous writing and efforts to amuse are usually painful to read, so better avoid them.

Abbreviations in essays
You must avoid all short forms like **can't**, **won't** and **isn't** and write the words out in full. The first time you use an acronym you should spell it out, for example 'The Organisation of Petroleum Exporting Countries (OPEC)...' after that you can use the acronym alone.

Trying to impress by complexity
Technical jargon is usually essential at university and makes for precision in communication. However you should not deliberately set out to write long, complex sentences or use less obvious words on the grounds that this is suitable for university level work. Too often arcane words are used incorrectly, your meaning becomes obscure, and you will lose marks. Even though your analysis may be complex the expression of it should be simple and clear.

Using brackets
These (when used often) tend to give (at least to some people) a feeling of choppiness (or breathlessness) and slow down the communication of ideas (or anything else).

The shotgun technique
This consists of throwing in everything you know about the issue in the hope that a few pellets will strike home, rather than answering the question.

Solution
Practise making skeleton answers; spend longer on organising your approach; stick to your prepared skeleton answer; keep reading the question as you write and use a few words from it now and then.

Getting sidetracked
This means moving away from the central question asked and delving into interesting but scarcely relevant areas. An assessor may think you have a scatty mind and a less than fully logical approach.

Solution
Use the same solution as for the shotgun technique.

Producing lightweight work

Skimpy, lightweight work lacks thorough research and full preparation – it may have been rushed off at the last minute!

Solution
Start preparing earlier; search longer for information and read more; discuss with your study-buddy; think and plan for longer.

Badly organised work

Badly organised work may well have been researched properly but the information hasn't been put together efficiently and therefore the question won't have been answered.

Solution
Practise making skeleton answers regularly; try to make several different ones for the same question; practise competitive skeleton answers with your study-buddy/group.

Careless work

This includes things like misspellings, ungrammatical English, use of incorrect words (like 'their' instead of 'there'), and repetitions.

Solution
Use a spell-checker on the computer; try a grammar checker (although they are still primitive); when finished, leave your paper to one side – read it over carefully later and make your corrections (white-out helps); try harder and take more care.

Unbalanced answers

This is where, for example, you have covered the cases for and against as asked, but argued the case *for* in six lines and spent the next six pages arguing the case against it.

Solution
Compare the number of points in your skeleton answer; compare the amount written for each section.

Sexist language

Avoid using *he* when referring to a professional person or role model as it could well be a *she*.

Solution
Try putting it in the plural – 'Doctors' then becomes 'they' later. You

can also use 's/he'.
Here is a short list of some words to avoid and their preferred
alternatives. Also, ask your university women's group if they have a list
you can have.

Not liked	Preferred
Actress	Actor
Authoress	Author
Chairman	Chair/chairperson
Gentlemen's agreement	Handshake agreement
Man and wife	Partners/husband and wife
Man hours	Work time/person hours
Man made	Artificial/synthetic
Poetess	Poet
Workman	Worker

Personal answers
There is room for your personal opinion, but avoid scattering 'I'
throughout the essay.

Solution
You might choose to restrict 'I' to the conclusion; go through looking
for 'I's' when finished and get rid of most of them.

Using 'ought', 'should' and 'must'
At university you are expected to be logical, analytical, creative and
scientific. Words like 'ought' are too personal and prescriptive.

Solution
Rephrase it: 'In order to achieve X the government could (might)...'

Using extreme language
If you keep saying **extremely, very, tremendously, enormously** or
remarkably you are probably overstating your case; if you use any of
the following you are definitely doing so.

alarmingly	unbelievably	grotesquely	staggering
meteoric	stupendous	disastrous	catastrophic
huge	vast	unprecedented	astronomical

Solution
Think about what you really believe and choose your words more

carefully; use a thesaurus; read over at the end and change any extreme words.

Personifying countries and institutions
You are better off not saying **she** for France or **they** for an organisation; these are things and really call for **it**.

Reaching conclusions without evidence
Believing something to be true is not evidence, nor is the fact that one book says so – another book may say the reverse.

Solution
Be sure you provide enough evidence for your conclusions; keep an eye open for spurious correlations or any hidden third causes – if statistics suggest that changes in the number of children born in Sweden vary with the number of storks breeding on one lake, we cannot assume that storks bring babies!

Labelling people or ideas
It is fairly easy to hang a label around the neck of someone of whom we disapprove and tarnish them with a poor image. 'Fascist' is regularly and incorrectly used as a critical description in this way. Equally the 'straw person' approach is suspect: here one defends a person in a deliberately weak way, then knocks down the defence with gusto. This can be fun, but does not produce balanced, quality work.

Solution
Don't do it!

Political or cultural bias
This is hard to spot in one's one work, but easier in the writings and statements of others. Common forms of bias are political, racial, social, and religious.

Solution
Watch for it carefully; ask your study-buddy if s/he notices anything like this about you.

Rambling answers
If you cannot keep to set length guidelines or your essays are much longer than other peoples' you are probably rambling. Markers' comments might indicate it also.

Solution
Take more care with skeleton answers; prune heavily; never repeat statements you have already made; avoid 'As I said before...' which means repetition.

ESSAY TIPS – THINGS TO FOLLOW

Taking care with quotations
Be particularly careful with questions that involve quotations. Be on guard if you see a quotation. It can indicate a tricky question, or the quote may be only partially true, or true only under certain circumstances. It may require you to adopt a critical approach.

Keeping measurements consistent
Stick either to metric or imperial measures. For example, do not use feet and inches in one part of your paper and then metres and millimetres in another. Similarly, do not mix fractions and percentages when making comparisons.

Plural and singular
If your subject is plural the verb form must also be plural; this applies however much the two may be separated in a long sentence: 'The country... are..' is just wrong.

Solution
Read over carefully at the end.

Adding a bibliography
You may be asked for a bibliography, but if not put one in anyway. It tends to impress the marker and shows you are trying hard.

Wait 24 hours
Before handing in your essay it is a good idea to wait a day and read it again for the final polishing and corrections. What seemed perfect yesterday can often be improved and gain you extra marks.

Photocopying
If you wrote it by hand or typed it, make sure you photocopy it before handing it in. Essays do get lost and it is a major hassle having to rewrite the whole thing or try to persuade the university you put it in. A photocopy brings peace of mind. If you wrote it on a computer, as advised, you need not bother to copy it as you have it on file and a back up.

Ongoing writing problems

If you still have writing problems ask if your university provides help. Some universities have an essay adviser, or similar, whose job is to provide help to those who have trouble writing. If your university provides this service, make an appointment and take a marked essay or two along to show and discuss your problems.

There are also books available to help with essay writing. Try for instance *Your Own Words* by Judith Wainwright and Jackie Hutton (Nelson, 1992) which some find helpful. See also the further reading section at the end of this book.

IMPROVING YOUR STYLE

This is not easy to do, nor will it happen quickly, but for long-term gains you can:

Practise writing a little each day

Like most things, good writing comes with practice, it does not just happen. Choose a topic and write about it for perhaps 15 minutes. Select each word with care and try to make your choice of words reflect exactly what you think and feel. Aim for economy of words and simplicity of expression. Use as few adjectives and adverbs as possible, and make the nouns and verbs do the work. If the topic is relevant to your university work, keep the piece of paper on file.

Do not keep using the same word

Avoid using a word twice in the same sentence or in close proximity. If you can't think of a substitute look in a thesaurus for one.

Reading more

Reading poetry and good modern novels steeps you in stylish writing and word use. How do you find good novels? The annual nominations for the Booker prize around November in the UK are considered well written novels. You can also ask in your Humanities or English department which will advise you on some modern novels to read. With a poem you should read it several times looking for the main meaning and any hidden ones. Examine each word and its relationship to the words around. The adjectives and adverbs chosen often particularly merit attention. Think about why each word was chosen – and see if you can find a word you like better.

HANDING ASSIGNMENTS IN ON TIME

You may lose marks if you **hand an assignment in late** and eventually it will not be accepted for marking. Furthermore, once you put in one late assignment, you tend to fall behind with the next. It is then hard to catch up and a depressing chain begins. In your rush to finish, don't forget to put your name and subject on the assignment, and anything else required – like the course code or marker's name.

Managing your time badly

If bad time management was responsible make a new and improved weekly timetable. You can also flag assignments earlier in your diary. **Think positive!** You are learning the valuable skill of time management that you obviously needed.

However, it may have been that you were afraid of the assignment and put off starting to prepare it. Never let fear crush you and stop you beginning. See the section on starting an assignment in Chapter 5.

Running late

If you are running late with an assignment, you can try asking for an extension, but make sure you have a good reason ready. Not being organised is not good enough, but sickness is usually and family problems might be. Ask early enough so that if your request is refused you can submit something, however quickly and badly written. It will get you some marks at least, whereas no submission gains you no marks at all.

For the long term, try to work more efficiently and/or increase your hours of study. See Figure 6 which will give you some idea of the way marking systems translate from percentages into grades. Individual institutions will vary, however, for example not all have a grade of 'pass conceded'. You should ask about the system and its actual meaning at your university.

CASE STUDIES

Alan is disappointed with his mark

Alan wants a high mark. After a shaky start, he now does adequate preparation but when writing if a new idea pops into his mind he builds on it, temporarily ignoring the planned outline. He then returns to his plan, causing the essay to lose some of its logical structure. He types it up quickly and leaves a few uncorrected spelling errors. He receives a mark of C+ and is disappointed. He promises himself that next time he will stick with the planned outline and work to avoid careless mistakes.

GRADE	MEANING	GRADE	PERCENTAGE
HD	High Distinction	A+ +	About 85%
D	Distinction	A- to A +	About 75%
C	Credit	B- to B + +	About 65%
P	Pass	C- to C + +	About 50%
PC	Pass conceded	D+ +	About 48%
F	Fail	D	Under 48%

Fig. 6. Typical marking systems with approximate grade equivalents.

Jane is pleased with her excellent mark

Jane also wants a top mark. She discussed the question with her study-buddy, organises several skeleton answers and digs out much information. When writing up she sticks faithfully to her outline. She adopts a tight, analytical approach and provides her own insights as well as the standard textbook answer. She uses a computer to write and print and gets a mark of A++. She is delighted.

Bob's mark reflects his effort

Bob only wants passing grades. He left it to the last minute to begin the essay, read his lecture notes, looked at one book, then wrote the answer from his head, without much planning. He also used unexplained abbreviations and his handwriting was not easy to read. His mark was a fail but only just, and his department decided to award a 'pass conceded'. This shook him a bit and he feels determined to work harder, start earlier, and prepare better next time.

DISCUSSION POINTS

1. What sort of writing habits could reduce your marks?

2. Write down as many words as you can think of in five minutes that can have a sexist connotation. What substitute words can you think of for each?

3. Have you ever been late with a school assignment or job at work? Why was that? How did you explain being late? Can you invent three better reasons?

SUMMARY

- Write assignments on a computer and print them; avoid handwritten essays if possible.

- Make sure you know what you think before you start to write.

- Answer the question asked and do not get sidetracked.

- Avoid slang, colloquial English, and attempts at humour.

- Avoid abbreviations, lots of brackets, and mixing units of measurement.

- Do not strive for complex sentences or use particularly obscure words.

- Analyse, rather than describe.

- Do not put down all you know about the issue.

- Organise your work clearly and balance your answer.

- Avoid sexist language, too personal answers, and extreme words.

- Avoid reaching conclusions without good evidence or labelling ideas for a cheap shot.

- Keep a copy of your assignments.

- Put your assignments in on time.

8
Doing Examinations

You should try to revise regularly throughout the term – set aside time every day to do a little. Half an hour is often enough, but it depends on your personality, your memory, your enthusiasm and so on. Good revision technique is to read your notes and make skeleton answers to questions from old exam papers, tutorials, the textbook and the study guide.

You will probably have a short break between the end of teaching and the beginning of your exams. Use this time wisely – this is your last chance for revision so you should make the most of it.

PREPARING FOR THE EXAM

Avoiding emotional upsets
This is a rotten time to choose to break off with a boyfriend or girlfriend, so if there is a danger of this happening, you should try to do so a lot earlier or wait until after the exams. Nothing should disturb your mental equilibrium, and emotional conflicts are high on the list of things that can pull down the standard of your work.

Making a plan
Try making a plan for the best use of your time. Allocate roughly equal time for each subject but make sure you give more to your weakest area. This can improve your overall performance, because it is generally easier to raise your mark from 40 to 50 per cent than from 70 to 80 per cent.

Breaking up study time
Break your study day into small chunks. Remember to work for your optimal length of time, whatever that is, and then take a break.

Reading your notes
You should spend time reading your notes and old skeleton answers to questions. For most people it is better to do this topic by topic. You should also go through your textbook and read the highlighted pieces and practise drawing diagrams.

Avoiding new work

It is a waste of time going to the library looking for new information or reading up new things at this late stage. This is pure revision time!

Practising answering questions

You can keep drawing up skeleton answers, alternating with reading your notes, textbook and existing skeleton outlines and discussing with your study-buddy.

Revising with others

It is good to work with your study-buddy or group for part of each day, either discussing topics or going through questions and brainstorming answers. Play games for variety. With a topic, you might all read it up from notes for say 10 minutes, then one explains it to the others, and they question, criticise and comment. Three topics and a short break often seem to work well. With a question, you can select one and discuss a possible answer. Alternatively each person could draft a skeleton answer for 5 minutes and compare it with the others. A really good composite answer can be devised from these efforts. All such group work makes a change from reading and studying on your own and helps you to remember.

The night before the exam

It is best to leave the night before an examination free. The little bit you will manage to stuff in your memory can be smaller than the amount you knock out. It is best to relax, which will help you sleep.

SITTING THE EXAM

Getting there

A few days before the exam, check the date, time and room are correct so that you do not inadvertently get there half an hour late or on the wrong day. The night before, make sure you set your alarm so you wake up in good time and avoid hassles and worries. Do not try to study before you leave. Eat something and get there in good time. If you go in by bus, you might catch the one earlier, just to be sure. If you have an ancient car that won't always start, consider getting a lift or choosing another more reliable way of getting there. When you get there, don't stand around discussing with friends possible questions and their answers. This process, like revising the night before, can be counter-productive. It can also start you worrying which you definitely do not need.

PRE-EXAM CHECKS THE DAY BEFORE

- Am I sure that I know where the room is and the time the exam starts? ☐

- Have I set a reliable alarm clock and maybe asked others to wake me as well? ☐

- Do I have coloured pens (not red), pencils, eraser, ruler, correcting fluid, a calculator, and a watch to take into the exam room? ☐

- Is my transport reliable? ☐

- Can I get there in time if something goes wrong? ☐

Fig. 7. A checklist for the day before your exam.

Taking your kit in with you

You should take a spare pen, some coloured pens or pencils if you expect to have a draw diagrams, an eraser, a ruler, some white-out liquid, a calculator if you might need one, and a reliable watch. If your native language is not English, a dictionary can be of help. Knowing you have all you might need can help reduce tension.

Use Figure 7 to help you check that you are prepared for the day of exam.

Once in the exam room

Go into the exam room as soon as you are allowed, find a seat where you will be comfortable, lay out your kit and **relax**. Use one of the quick relaxation techniques if you feel the need. When you are allowed to do so, read the instructions carefully, and do everything they tell you. Read through the questions several times, select which ones you will tackle, and mark them with a tick or number. Ignore all the other questions henceforth. Reading them again is a waste of time and can make you feel worried. You must attempt the required number of questions – check again to make sure you are not doing too few or too many. With a multi-part question, make sure you answer all the parts.

Dividing your time

It is best to divide your time up between questions and allow say 15 minutes for reading over at the end. Give each question the same time unless one question is worth more marks, in which case give it more time. Pace yourself when writing – four questions of decent length and reasonably done usually earn more marks than three voluminous ones and a few scrappy lines for the fourth. If you are running late, the last question can often be done in note form and will normally get you some marks.

Making skeleton outlines
Making skeleton outlines is not *time wasted* but *time invested* – good answers get good marks. Good answers include the basic elements, organised in logical fashion, and written up legibly. This will not happen by accident; if you seize your pen and start writing madly, you should anticipate not getting a good mark. Ignore the idiot next to you who does that. Read the question carefully both *before* and *as* you make the skeleton answer.

Remember also to **answer the question asked**. No 'Before I deal with this . . .' beginnings please!

Using subheads
In many subjects, good use of subheads, underlined but not in red, help you gain marks. However, a few courses, like English literature and foreign languages, may not allow them. Subheads make your outline stand out so that the assessor can rapidly see the logic of your approach and extent of your knowledge. It is particularly good if your handwriting is poor, because it makes marking easier and this pleases the one person who decides how many marks you will get.

Starting your main answer
Do not waste time writing out the words of the question – just put its number in the margin. Your introduction should be short and the start of your main text ought to be on the first page. Unless instructed otherwise, start a new page for each question; the paper does not cost you anything and the marker can find new questions more easily.

Writing legibly
Try your hardest to write legibly. If no one can read it, expect no marks. If only parts of it can be read, you will only get some marks. Do not use a red pen either, for writing or diagrams – the last thing you need is to irritate the marker.

Using diagrams
In many disciplines, assessors like to see diagrams and they can get you

marks. You need not waste time making your diagrams works of art – as long as diagrams are neat (use a ruler) and correct it is enough. Depending on your subject, one diagram per question is not too much, and more might be necessary. Make sure you label all the parts of the diagram properly.

Crossing out the extras

You should clearly cross out any plan skeletons, diagrams, or notes that you do not want marked. No sane marker ever reads more than necessary!

> Keep in mind all the essay tips in Chapter 7.

Avoiding exam post-mortems

It is a mistake to hang around outside the exam room discussing the paper you just answered which only helps to maintain or even increase your level of stress. You need to forget the exam you just did and relax, ready for the next one ahead.

PREPARING FOR OTHER EXAM FORMATS

This section looks at alternative forms of testing including:

- multiple choice quizzes
- write-in answers
- true–false tests.

Multiple choice quizzes are increasingly being used in tertiary level education. This is not because they are thought to be intrinsically better than essay-style exams but because they are the natural, if ugly, offspring of governments trying to get education on the cheap. Student numbers have increased but government money has not: without a proportional increase in staff, quicker forms of assessment and marking have to be used. The use of computers has speeded up multiple choice marking considerably and in many disciplines you now need to know how to cope with multiple choice tests and exams.

You should check recent exam papers and your course syllabus to see what type of quiz will be set and practise it. Your textbook or study guide may have examples – and there is a chance the course convenor will choose from those questions too which will give you an edge.

Improving your multiple choice scores

Choosing the 'best' answer
With all multiple choice quizzes you select the best answer from the
choices offered. This is the one that applies normally or covers the most
options. See the following question.

A sea gull is:	☐
(a) A bird.	☐
(b) A large bird.	☐
(c) A large bird that eats fish.	☐
(d) None of the above.	☐

The best answer is C, even if A and B are correct, because it covers
the most. There is never any point writing annotations on multiple
choice papers explaining your choice, because no one reads them.
Writing 'Some gulls eat inland and never see a fish' and choosing B,
gets you a wrong mark.

Moving on if stuck
If you cannot answer a particular question you should go immediately
to the next one and not waste time fretting over one that seems
particularly difficult. There will probably be others later than you can
answer. You must finish the paper if you are to score the highest mark
you can. When you reach the end, go back to the ones that you missed
earlier and start again, and keep going until you finish or time runs out.

Drawing yourself a diagram
With some questions it may help you to understand them if you draw a
diagram to work out what is happening. The back of the question
paper and inside back cover of the exam paper are good places, but
cross the diagram out before handing your paper in.

Taking care with tricky questions
Negative questions ('Which of the following is not a cause...') can be
tricky. You might find it helps to remove the negative, ask yourself which
is a cause and cross them off, which leaves the correct answer exposed.

Dealing with the 'All of the above' and 'None of the above' choices can also be tricky. If you decide that one offered choice cannot be true, you know 'All the above' must be wrong and can be eliminated. If two choices contradict or are mutually incompatible, again it cannot be correct. With 'none of the above', if you can determine that a single choice works then you can eliminate the 'none' answer.

Always guess rather than leave blanks
Most universities give a mark for a correct answer but do not subtract a mark for a wrong one. If yours is like this, it means you maximise your score by guessing those you cannot work out. If you guess you *might* be right; if you fail to answer you *must* be wrong. To improve the odds, before you blindly guess, see if you can eliminate one or two of the choices and choose between the remainder.

Using the essay questions to help
When stuck, you can sometimes work out the correct multiple choice answer by looking at the essay questions, the write-in questions or even other multiple choice questions on the paper as these might offer clues.

It is always worth checking the lengths of the choices offered. Sometimes (but definitely not always) the correct answer is indicated by the longest choice offered.

Improving your score for write-in answers

Reading all the questions first
It is probable that questions for **write-in tests** will be chosen from different parts of the course to get a good coverage. If a later question simply *must* be about topic X then an earlier question is perhaps less likely to be. So do not rush straight in and fill in the early ones before reading all the questions. Again, possible overlap means that valuable clues to write-in tests may lie elsewhere on the paper.

Choosing the right words
There may be several, probably lots, of different phrases and words that will fit the gaps. For instance 'When the level of ... increases we expect to see a ... in national income or an increase in ...' In an economics exam the words 'demand', 'rise' and 'inflation' would be required but in a geography one, 'flood water', 'change' and 'waterborne diseases' would fit. Do not panic but choose sensible words that suit the course you are doing.

Scoring well on the creative write-in questions
With questions like 'Write down as many uses of a pencil you can think of', you are expected to demonstrate creativity, lateral thinking and inventiveness. You should aim to think of really original things in addition to the obvious ones. Everyone will say 'Writing letters' but you should add uses like 'constructing a see-saw for tame mice', 'using it to cast the shadow in a sundial', or 'giving it to a garden gnome to add a professional air' and similar creative and off-beat uses. You should not worry about being silly or looking foolish, because suggesting amusing uses actually tends to gain you marks. Write down as many as you can in the time allowed. If the write-in is part of a general exam and you have time left over, go back to this section and keeping inventing new uses.

Improving your score in true–false tests

Assuming the answer is right
Never get too clever and think the statement is usually true but under a special set of circumstances it would be false and select that one. The *obvious* answer is most usually correct in true–false tests. The really tricky questions tend to be asked in the essay section.

Asking yourself 'what would happen if?'
If you are unsure, think through what would happen if it were true, and what would happen if it were false. Considering these implications, choose the set that seem most reasonable.

Drawing a diagram
It sometimes helps to draw a diagram to work out what is going on.

Guessing
When you really have no idea at all, always **guess**. Remember: unanswered questions get you no marks but marks are rarely deducted for wrong answers in this type of test.

Avoiding balancing your answers
The setters do not have a 50 per cent rule, so there is never any point in adjusting your answers to get an equal number of 'yes' and 'no' ones. Multiple choice answers are similarly random and do not have one quarter allocated to each A, B, C and D answer.

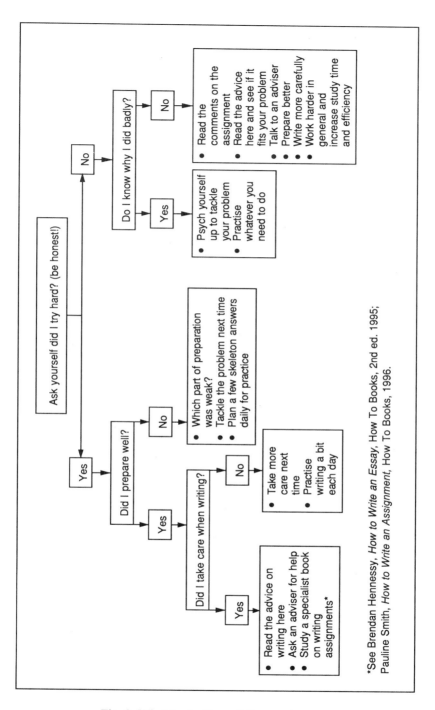

Fig. 8. What to do if you fail an assignment.

101

UNDERSTANDING WHY CHEATING IS STUPID

It may be tempting to try to smuggle notes or a piece of information into the exam room on your ruler, in a pencil case, or programmed into a calculator but **do not bother**. Rarely does your mark rely on you knowing a few facts, dates, symbols, *etc.* The mark you get tends to reflect the overall quality of your answer, judged by, for example, the standard of your arguments, the logical way you tackle the question, and the weight of the evidence you use. The rewards for successful cheating are often surprisingly small. The risks are great and you might be given zero for the exam. Should you succeed in cheating, you still do not know how well you are really doing.

If you are unlucky enough to fail an assignment study Figure 8 to help you assess where you went wrong and what you can do to remedy it next time.

CASE STUDIES

Alan's steady revision pays off now
Alan is scared facing his first exam after being away from study for over a decade, but knows he has revised consistently so he should be all right. His enthusiasm takes over and he does not spend enough time selecting the questions carefully. He plans his answers but not as well as he might. He has a spare pen but no white-out and his corrected paper looks messy with crossings out. He gets a B but had hoped for an A.

Jane sees the exam as an exciting challenge
Jane looks forward to the exam but keeps this fact quiet. She knows she will do well and has revised steadily over the whole term. She takes a full kit in, chooses the questions carefully and plans them out. She gets an A + and is happy.

Bob's fear is common
Bob panicked before the exam when he realised he had done no revision. He revised like mad for three days staying up late and is really tired on the day. He has no kit and does not plan his answers before writing. His pen runs out and he has to finish in pencil. His borderline fail is not bad enough to get him thrown out but another one could doom him.

DISCUSSION POINTS

1. If you have four subjects and seven days in which to revise them,

how would you organise your revision schedule? Why?

2. What might you do if you get to the exam room far too early? What would not be a good idea?

3. Would you agree that with a limited amount of time in the exam room, you should start writing immediately after selecting the questions you will answer? Can you defend your position?

SUMMARY

- Most of your revision should be done steadily throughout the term.

- Make a plan for the best use of your final revision time.

- In the revision period you should refuse to do any new work.

- It helps to vary your activity when revising.

- Working with your study-buddy or group makes a good and useful change.

- Get to the exam room early, take a kit, and settle in a comfortable place.

- Allocate your time carefully between questions.

- Always plan out your answer before you start to write.

- Answer the question asked.

- Use subheads if it is allowed.

- Write legibly, do not use red, but do use diagrams where appropriate.

- With multiple choice quizzes do not get hung up on one question.

- Take special care with negative multiple choice questions.

- Unless wrong answers are penalised, guess rather than leave a blank, but eliminate what options you can first.

- When stuck, read the other questions and look at the length of the option for help.

- With write-in answers, read all the questions before filling in answers and be creative with open ended invention questions.

- With true–false questions, ask 'what would happen if...', draw a diagram if it helps, and guess if you have to.

- Do not try to cheat!

9
Developing Team Skills

Some of the skills increasingly being sought in business include the ability to:

- communicate well
- solve problems
- organise tasks in order of priority
- manage time properly
- exercise leadership
- take initiatives
- work successfully in a team.

The days of a job for life have virtually disappeared and many people now work for a few years on contract before moving on. You will need portable skills to cope with the changing times. When you are in a job, you are likely to find yourself working in a team undertaking a project and when it is over the team will disband. You might then join a different team to tackle something new.

WORKING IN A TEAM

Some university courses require you to undertake a group project, while others offer you the chance if you want it. Even if you are committed to studying a particular discipline, it is worth seeing if you can take a course perhaps from another field or department which allows team work. The skills you will learn will be of great help in finding a job and furthering your career.

Working in a team you will start to develop not only the above skills but others such as:

- understanding group dynamics
- working in cooperation with others
- delegating responsibility
- smoothing ruffled feathers

- building in safety margins for deadlines
- editing the work of others
- combining individual documents into one report.

STARTING YOUR PROJECT

There will probably be a staff member present who might either tell you what to do, or take a 'resources' role, so you can ask questions and get help when you need it. However, they may only volunteer information if it seems to them you desperately need it.

Choosing the right leader

A mature experienced student is often the best but a good 18-year-old is always better than a hopeless 30-year-old. The entire group can sit and talk about who might make a good leader but in the end you may have to take a volunteer. If an existing study group is the nucleus of your team you will already know each other's strengths and can choose a good leader. The leader's job is to organise and control without offending people, smooth over disputes that might arise, maybe liaise with the staff member, and be able to write well.

Brainstorming: throwing initial ideas around

Unless a staff member suggests something different try a **brainstorming** session to consider the main points that might be addressed. It helps to consider the different ways the question might be tackled. A good way is to discuss this in small groups of maybe four to eight students for five to ten minutes, then one member from each group gets up and reports what the group concluded. You should get several decent and different ideas in this way. If you write the suggestions and ideas on the board as you go, you should eventually get agreement on the best approach by a process of mixing and matching.

Making a timetable

You should make a rough **timetable** so that everyone knows when things are due. The following stages are typical:

- **Stage one**: running a brainstorming session to decide how to tackle the question, which you are doing now and hopefully will be finished in one meeting.

- **Stage two**: the small teams research their own part and put together a team report which goes up to the main group.

- **Stage three**: writing the draft (main) report.

- **Stage four**: examining the draft report, deciding on changes, and then writing the final report.

- **Stage five**: presenting the final report in a full session and then submitting it.

It is desirable to incorporate a few safety margins on dates, so that if anyone is late (and somebody will be!) it does not delay the final report.

WORKING IN SMALL GROUPS

Dividing the task into parts
Once you have the broad approach agreed and have broken down the question into its main sections, you can divide into teams. One team is needed for each main part of the skeleton and each team may consist of between two and eight students. If some parts seems likely to be more difficult you could make that team larger. Often teams emerge naturally, as friends wish to work together.

Each team needs a leader
Someone should be in charge, to raise issues like when and where the members will next meet, and who might go with whom to search for what, who will liaise with other teams, and pull things together and make sure the team report gets finished. People probably need to know who is in charge of each team. The teams meet separately and first decide what each member is going to investigate. You should arrange a date for when your team will next meet to report progress, and then a date for the final information to come together. It is a good idea to build in a safety margin of a few days or a week before you must hand over your findings to the whole group.

Liaising with other teams
Your team might need to talk to some of the other teams to ensure that you are roughly agreeing on direction and beliefs. It might be embarrassing if four other teams decide the project is good and yours believes it is bad and your report seriously clashes with the others. However, it is not always essential to liaison, and to some extent it depends on the topic and the individuals involved.

Writing the small group report
Each member of the team will probably need to draft out a report on individual findings which can be in note form for convenience. The team should meet to discuss these and iron out any obvious

contradictions as well as determine the major thrust that the team report will take. Someone, probably the team leader, has to take all the notes and write up one report from them. Your team might wish to meet again to see it or might decide to trust the leader.

ASSEMBLING THE OVERALL GROUP REPORT

Deciding who will do it
The draft report is usually best put together by the group leader after consultations, either with two to four main people or with the leaders of all the small teams. A committee is unsuitable for creative writing and is best used for guidelines and suggesting amendments.

Writing the report
The group leader first reads the reports of all the small teams, and gets an idea of the overall thrust of the views. It is often wise to talk to the team leaders at this stage. Second, the leader examines the original outline from the first brainstorming session and decides if that is still valid as a result of the findings. If so, the shape of the report is established. If not, then some tinkering with the outline will be needed. The leader then sits and edits, cuts and pastes, and rewrites as necessary, until one coherent and non-contradictory report emerges.

A draft conclusion and introduction may also be prepared at this stage. Many people find it easier to write the introduction last, after the conclusion.

Approving the draft report
The draft report, along with the introduction and conclusion, can be circulated to all for their comments if there is time. Otherwise it will have to be read out at a full meeting. You do *need* this approval – you do not want the members of a small group standing up later and denying the parts of the report they were responsible for! You will probably find you need some changes, and perhaps significant compromises will be required. If the topic allows for differences of political opinion, this can be a stormy stage.

WRITING AND DELIVERING THE FINAL REPORT

Only one person can really write the final report and it will probably be the task of the overall leader unless someone who is known to write particularly well can be persuaded to do it. It may be required by the rules of the course that this report be presented and discussed at a plenary session. Otherwise it might be submitted directly for assessment. If considered in a full meeting, it is often a good idea to let the heads of the small team present the part of the final report they researched earlier. This keeps them happy and involved (job satisfaction) and as the experts they will be able to handle any questions which arise, better than anyone else.

BEING AWARE OF POTENTIAL PROBLEMS

Group projects take more effort than ordinary assignments and take longer than you might think. The following are a few of the problems that may arise and which you should watch out for.

1. Problems of authority and control versus democratic participation may arise.

2. Differences in political or social views can sometimes make compromise difficult.

3. The progress of the overall group can be no faster than its slowest part.

4. There are new skills to be learned and this takes time.

Possible coordination problems
- Within a small team, some individuals may be slower than others.

- One or more small teams may put their report in late.

- There may be noticeable quality differences between the reports from the small groups.

- The report of one small team may contradict the reports of others – this requires the political skills of mediation and compromise to solve.

- Some may object to the thrust or conclusions of the overall draft report – solving this problem requires the same political skills.

Dealing with a poor leader
If the leader you have chosen initially turns out to be hopeless, it can be painful to try and change later. There is a lot of face involved and it may be easier to live with a poor leader and provide support by means of a small advisory group who will do the real work.

Allocating marks
Allocating marks fairly can present problems. It is tempting to give

equal marks to the members of the group or small team. However, some will have taken on more responsibility and done more to organise, control, write, and liaise with others. They will probably feel they should get more marks. There is no easy solution and you can spend a lot of time discussing and trying to sort out a fair distribution without obvious success.

Coping with free-riders

One or two people may sign up for the course, turn up a few times then after that do little work, yet get an equal share of the marks. This is not only unfair, it is resented by the hard workers who carry them. Frankly, little can be done, apart from ensuring people know who these free-riders are. The overall leader could have a word with them but it rarely seems to work. Peer group pressure could be tried but such people are often impervious. Getting a fair distribution of marks related to both effort and output can also be extremely difficult. In the short term free-riders appear to win: they get marks for little or no work. In the long run they are losers: they do not develop the skills they need, they lose friends, get a bad reputation, and they learn little about the subject matter.

> With group projects, be prepared to work hard. There is a steep learning curve involved and such projects can take more time and effort than you might imagine.

CASE STUDIES

Alan is a good team leader

Alan is very good at group work – he is chosen as the overall leader and is part of one team as well, which he takes over when the leader is ill for a week and somehow keeps the position. He manages to diffuse a situation where two leaders of small teams were at loggerheads and keep them both happy. He writes up the overall report on his own and gives it to two others to edit which improves it further.

Jane learns how to work in a team

Jane is used to working on her own and despite benefiting from finding a study-buddy, she lacks the skills to work well with a larger group. She is a poor performer at first and finds it hard to trust the other members of her group to do their bit properly. She does well going off on her own to dig up information, and the notes she puts together are excellent – but she cannot argue persuasively in discussion. Her team members know how well she scores in essay writing and she is talked into writing up her team findings, which she does ably. She feels happy about that and has begun to feel that she belongs in the team. She makes several new friends out of the experience.

Bob enjoys being part of a team

Bob does surprisingly well. Early on he was tempted to goof off and be a free-rider but to his surprise he actually got interested in the topic and ended up working hard with several friends. When some of his suggestions were adopted he felt particularly good about it. He is beginning to think he might join a study group if team work can be fun like this and make learning less painful.

DISCUSSION POINTS

1. What sort of job would you like after you graduate? What skills can you gain from participating in team projects that would help you get and keep that job?

2. Have you ever worked on a team project or with a partner before? Did you research separately or together? Did you write up separately or together? What did you learn from the experience? Would you do it differently next time?

3. If you had the problem of a free-rider in a group project, how could you tackle it? Which way would you try first?

SUMMARY

- Get involved in a group project if you can.
- At the first session, choose a leader, get an outline adopted and make a timetable.
- Set up small teams, one for each section of the outline.
- Each team researches a clearly defined area and reports up.
- The leader and a few others make a draft report which has to be agreed.
- A final report is written and approved by all, probably in full session, then submitted.
- Problems of a poor leader, coordination, and free-riders may arise.
- Group projects need much work and time.

10
Developing Role-Playing Skills

DEVELOPING LIFE SKILLS

As part of your university career, even if you are dedicated to your preferred discipline, you should seriously consider doing at least one subject which involves role-playing. These might be located in the university's commerce or business faculty and many universities now allow you to cross-register. Check the university handbook or ask in the department or faculty office. The experience and skills you gain can give you the edge when you are looking for a job and will stand you in good stead for the rest of your life. Role-playing courses require effort because you have to work on both content and presentation for top marks. You will develop the skill to:

- research a practical project which is closer to business, government and commercial needs
- develop your own individual approach to a problem
- improve your communication
- promote your persuasive capacity
- enhance your self-confidence
- organise complex material in new ways
- creatively work out ways of using photographs, diagrams and other props
- put together a visually attractive and persuasive final report.

Role-playing sessions look good on your CV, can provide an interesting topic in an interview, and can help you secure a good job. If you get the opportunity, go for it!

Learning from others
It is tempting not to go to the presentations of others, when you have heaps of work to do, are struggling to define your topic clearly, and searching for elusive information. Resist this temptation! You should attend everybody else's sessions and watch, listen and learn from their

successes and failings. Consider carefully whatever criticisms and suggestions the staff member makes and see how you can incorporate them into your delivery. Unlike tutorials, if you have a choice it is better to do your presentation late in the term because by then you will have learned a lot from watching the others.

DEALING WITH ESSENTIALS

Timing
Make sure you know how long you have got in which to make your presentation. There will almost certainly be time taken out at the end for questions, discussion, and suggestions. Typically, an hour session will have maybe 20 minutes for your actual presentation, but in a half-hour session you would be lucky to get more than 15 minutes.

Getting there early
Get there early and check out the room, making sure all the equipment you need is there and working, lay out any props, and put up any maps, posters, or photographs you will use.

Dressing the part
You need to dress up in character to get your best performance: it will help you to do better and will also impress the student audience and staff member. Men should wear a suit and tie, women a business suit or plain blouse and dark skirt, and both need leather shoes – the whole power-dressing game in fact. Women should use make-up and simple jewellery like earrings – it all helps.

Using cards to present your talk
Do not write an essay and read it out – it is a recipe for disaster. Instead, put your notes on cards (which takes care of the problem of what to do with one hand), and glance at them for your next point. Keep your head up and go for maximum eye contact; keep sweeping the room, looking in eyes for a second or two and make sure you have eventually looked in everybody's eyes at least once. Keep the cards low and do not get them in front of your face. You should never place them on something flat to read, which loses your eye contact and points the top of your head at the audience. You can gesture with the cards for emphasis.

STARTING YOUR TALK

Setting the scene
Start by telling the audience who you are, who they are, why they are

here, what you want from them in general terms, and the title of your project. If your instructions do not state who the audience are supposed to be, you decide and tell them. Only when the scene is set should you begin your talk.

Starting the presentation

A good way is to pass out your handout. Make sure that your name, the project name, the date, and who the audience is supposed to be are on the front page. A good logo helps a lot too – design your own or use a computer word processor to import a suitable graphic. When passing out any material, make sure that if there is a leader of the group in the audience (the managing director of a company, leader of a delegation, President of Ruritania, *etc*), they get the item first.

Grabbing the audience's attention

Try to grab the attention of your audience at once, perhaps by some bold statement ('I hope to persuade you to invest US$20 million in a laboratory in Doncaster in the next ten minutes') or by drawing their attention to a particularly impressive poster or overhead transparency. A prop may help; for example, if you plan to sell doughnuts you might bring some along for people to try – hold them up and show them as a 'teaser' and tell them they can try them at the end. Such things add interest, get the attention of the audience, and earn marks for you.

PRESENTING YOURSELF WELL

Appealing to your audience

You will be standing out in front. Watch your posture and try to stand tall and look dominant. Do not lounge or lean on the furniture. Try to avoid:

- putting one or both hands in your pockets
- keeping your arms hanging permanently by your sides
- standing with your arms on your hips
- clenching your fists
- keeping your hands permanently behind your back.

You need to use gestures to put your points over. What to do with your hands is a perennial problem. As early in the term as you can, start watching speakers on TV, including politicians, games show presenters and entertainers, and concentrate on what they do with their hands and arms. Watch for particular gestures that accompany good news, underline a point to be emphasised, try to persuade, or diminish criticism. You can practise these in front of a mirror first in silence and then while speaking – the TV people you learned them from did this! See also the advice on body language in Chapter 6.

Being aware of your voice
Refer back to the advice on using your voice well in Chapter 6.

Making sure you are heard
Project your voice so that those in the back row can hear you. If you have a microphone, try to keep it at a steady distance from your mouth or you might fade suddenly. If it is fixed in one spot, do not move away from it when you speak and remember to go back to it to answer questions.

Avoiding nervous speech habits
Ask your friends if you have any bad speech habits – almost everyone seems to have some. In particular avoid incomprehensible noises like 'errr', 'erm' or 'um', and punctuating your sentences with words such as 'you know', 'right' or 'like'. You should avoid putting meaningless words on the end of sentences like 'Yeah', 'Hmm', 'So', 'OK?' or 'Right then'. If you have such a habit, it annoys people and they may start to listen for the noises, rather than to your message.

Repeating points for emphasis
If a point is really important and you wish to emphasise it, you can repeat the phrase when you are public speaking: 'We expect to earn 35 per cent by year two – that's 35 per cent!'. You must not use such repetition in a written essay of course.

USING VISUAL AIDS

Overhead transparencies
OHTs are virtually essential these days in universities although in the real world the use of computer presentation packages is replacing them. Prepare all your OHTs in advance and make sure they are large enough. Always use block capitals unless you have a specific reason not to. In my experience, more OHTs fail to work properly through being too small than for any other reason.

What to put on your OHT
- your talk outline (if not supplied as a handout)
- the data you will use
- any systems you will use
- all diagrams or charts you need
- maps or blueprints.

Tips for using OHTs

1. Leave them up, people need a long time to absorb things.

2. Do not keep turning the machine on and off.

3. Keep your OHTs simple.

4. Enlarge all your data if photocopied from a book or journal.

5. Only put up the bits of data you need, not huge tables containing figures you will not use.

6. Remember the data never explain themselves – tell us what they mean.

7. You must use colour; you can underline, highlight, or draw boxes, circles or arrows as you need and three colours are usually enough.

8. Do not change the colours unless you have a reason; and then say what it is.

9. Avoid green with red; orange with yellow; orange with brown; blue with green. They can be hard to distinguish.

10. Black goes with yellow or red but not with blue; red goes well with yellow.

11. You will need a 'key' to explain your different colours.

12. Number your OHTs in the order you will use them, in case you drop them.

13. It is best to make your main OHT different from your handout.

If you need to draw on an OHT you can do so easily by sliding it under the transparent roll or a blank transparency and drawing on that. This keep the OHT unmarked for use later.

Using the OHT machine
Well ahead of time make sure the room you will be using has a machine and that it is working.

• Make sure you know how to work the machine.

- Do not stand in front of the beam or block the view whilst using it; move if necessary.

Black - and whiteboards

If you have a choice, always use OHTs rather than blackboards; the latter are less effective and you have to turn your back on the audience.

Making sure you have the right pens or chalk
Check in advance to see if there is chalk (coloured if you need it) or proper whiteboard pens and an eraser. If not, take your own. Check the pens are designed for whiteboards because many pens designed for other purposes will not rub out, which irritates the university and you will also run out of space quickly.

Writing larger than normal
Write clearly using large letters to ensure the people at the back can read it easily. Try to keep your lines straight and if using a blackboard, do not make the chalk squeak!

Speaking up
When you turn your back to write, or to indicate something on the board, remember to project your voice more, because much of the sound disappears when you are not facing your audience.

Using video films

A short video film can be effective as long as it is central to your project. If it is long or peripheral it will most likely be a waste of your limited time.

USING PROPS

You need to use some props if you are to be fully effective. They grab people's attention, increase their interest and motivate them to listen to you. Some tips:

1. You can use representations of items, *eg* photographs, posters, handbills, and pictures.

2. You can use actual items themselves: a toy, dress material, food, whatever is appropriate. These tend to work better than representations but both are useful.

3. It is better not to put up a complex diagram in the first few minutes,

it can frighten people, but you might use graphs, diagrams and pictures to communicate information later in your talk.

4. Use your props as early as you can – a teaser particularly can work well – eg you *show* a prop early but use it fully later.

5. Try to get audience participation if you can: eg pass a prop round for them to taste, stroke, or examine.

MORE ROLE-PLAYING TIPS

Paying attention to detail
Make sure there are no spelling mistakes on OHTs or handouts; and 'principal' should not be 'principle', *etc.* Silly errors can cost you marks.

Staying in character
Once you begin, do not drop out of character. If a close friend asks a question, stay with your professional voice and manner.

Adopting a particular style
Consider the best style of presentation for you.

• 'Warm, knowledgeable and helpful' works well for many – it is good for extroverts.

• 'Cool, clear and scientific' is suitable for some – the quiet, introvert or the plain nervous may do better with this one.

• 'Friendly and amusing' is only for the few who are naturally witty.

• 'Shallow and superficial' – this is the danger if 'friendly and amusing' breaks down.

• 'Diffident and uncertain' is a bad style.

Coping with accidents
If you drop something what can you do?

• Ignore it – this often works well.

• Turn it to your advantage with a witty remark – almost always the best way if you can do it ('Whoops, one is escaping!').

• Shamble an apology and look remorseful. This is not a good idea, especially if you are naturally diffident, because it makes you look incompetent.

- Grovel around and pick it up. This can be irritating if people are forced to wait around.

- If you really need to use it later, pick it up as neatly and quickly as you can.

Coping with jocular remarks

It is usually best to totally ignore any teasing remarks from friends, which usually stops them. Only if you are witty and experienced at humorous put-downs should you think of responding. Otherwise a poor response is embarrassing, leaves a bad taste in the mouth, and can earn you a lower mark.

Stressing the positive

It is best not to knock your competitors by name whether these are companies, countries, political parties or alternative theories. It will probably irritate some of those present and in the real world the word might get back to the opposition! It is preferable to stress where your product, theory, *etc* is simply better.

1. Your product is lighter, smaller, more portable, cheaper, more durable, easier to maintain or fix, uses less fuel, does more, or runs faster – whatever you can think of.

2. Your theory explains more, needs fewer assumptions, fits alongside other theories more easily, predicts more accurately and fits the recent data better – again whatever you can think of.

3. Your party is closer to grass roots, more democratic, has splendid leaders or whatever.

Good words and phrases to use

– stimulating	– popular
– potential	– valuable
– safe	– dynamic
– active participation	– exciting prospects
– strategic plan	– actively investigating
– growth area	– excellent prospects

These tend to sound positive and encouraging. Notice that fashionable phrases come and go, so that not all of these might be desirable a decade hence and new ones will surely arise. Do not try to get too many in one presentation, or you might begin to sound over-confident or over-eager.

Measuring success

As well as explaining what you are **aiming** to do, you should decide how you will **measure success** in your particular project. You might be asked this as a question, even if it is not a part of your presentation. Another question which will be high in the mind of your audience is '**What do I get out of it?**'. Make sure you address that question as you go through your presentation. Depending on the nature of your project it might be things like:

- high profits to be made
- fast pay-off and quick returns
- new markets and high export earnings
- friends and contacts to be made
- enhancing the institution's good name
- company tax reduction
- higher national tax revenues
- minimal risk and high degree of safety
- a major breakthrough or discovery is likely
- winning more votes and getting elected
- attracting more students
- enlarging the size of your country.

Your concluding sentences

Your final words should sum up the project and remind the audience what exactly you want from them. It is polite to thank them for their attendance and attention. Then ask for questions if that is the norm for your course.

HANDLING QUESTIONS IN ROLE-PLAYING SESSIONS

Repeating the question

If you have a large room with many people, a question from near the front will be inaudible to those at the back. Repeat the question for the benefit of the audience.

Look at the questioner

Never look worried by the question. Get eye contact at once, look pleased, try to be positive and seem interested in the question.

Buying time

If it is a tricky question that you hadn't anticipated, you can try to buy time and make the questioner feel good with stalling phrases (see Chapter 6). An occasional slight pause (say, four to five seconds) while you think, is acceptable and it shows you are really considering the issue carefully. Don't do this for every question though – it tends to make you look dumb!

Using humour

If you are capable, you not only *can* but *should* use humour in your answer. This is often not a good idea in seminars, but it can work well in role-playing sessions.

Using your props

When answering a question, pick up and use a prop if you can. It interests the audience, impresses the staff member, and can be useful to deflect attention from the quality of your answer if it is weak.

Using positive language

Negative phrases are best avoided so try to find a substitute if you can. The aim is to be positive and sound as if you are in charge of events.

Negative phrases to avoid	Positive substitutes
I do not know	I will find out; all the data is not in yet but we will know shortly; my assistant is looking at that now (real world!); it is too soon to be certain but it looks as if...
Maybe; perhaps, could be	It certainly looks that way; we currently think that is the case; apparently; we suspect that...
I think you are wrong	The data actually suggest...
I guess so	Yes; that's right; absolutely; all the data suggest that is correct
I am trying to...	I will...
I think it was called...	A name like...
I have never been there (as an excuse)	All my research indicates
Somebody told me	It is believed in the industry
I've read in a book; I read somewhere	I believe; some suggest; one source indicated
Somewhere about there (pointing to a map)	Just here

If you are ever forced to admit ignorance, immediately say what you will do to correct this, eg 'I will find out and get the answer to you by close of business today'.

Ignore the staff member
Do not look at the staff member when you get a question, because it looks as if you are seeking help or sympathy, and may be in a bit of a panic.

CASE STUDIES

Alan makes an excellent presentation
Alan did well in a project concerned with establishing a medical clinic in a Third World country using overseas aid. He prepared a good handout and several OHTs using colour and originality of design. He dressed up properly in a suit and tie – and his drama talents showed. He immediately grabbed the audience using a plastic skull and a poster of a baby to talk about life expectancy. He used several interesting props, including a few medical implements his wife was able to borrow from the hospital where she works. He enjoyed the session and so did the audience; he got an excellent mark of A++.

Jane learns a lot from the experience
Jane did reasonably well despite her fears – she attended all the early presentations and listened to the advice of the staff member. Her project was about selling education in Britain to overseas students as a form of export earning. She prepared her handout and chose her props well. Her OHTs were well drawn and neat. She dressed up for it but her general lack of interest in clothes means that in the outside world she might look a bit dowdy. She used make-up which helped, but her diffidence showed in her low quiet voice and she could not look at individuals in the audience. The process terrified her but she got a decent B+. She learned a lot and feels next time she would do much better and get a B++ or even an A. She has begun to acquire skills that she rather desperately needs and actually got more from the course than anyone.

Not making an effort means low marks
Bob's project was about starting a new political party in Wales aiming at fighting the next general election. His presentation was not particularly good and he did not go to many of the earlier sessions. His handout had spelling errors and he forgot to put his name on it. His OHTs however were attractive and well designed with good colour,

which impressed the assessor, but he failed to use any props. He wore a jacket and tie but his trainers rather spoiled the effect. He learned a bit from the process of presentation, and got a mark of C+.

DISCUSSION POINTS

1. What sort of stance and gestures would not look good in a role-playing session? Do you tend to drift into using any of these? What can you do with your hands when speaking in public?

2. Quickly think of a project in your discipline or area. What really interesting first sentence can you invent to grab the attention of the audience?

3. What unsuitable words *ie* that can give a negative image would you avoid in a project about:
   (a) Selling motorcars.
   (b) Persuading overseas students to come to your university and pay for their education.
   (c) Persuading people to donate blood to hospitals.

SUMMARY

- Give your session late in the term if possible.

- Dress up for a better performance and marks.

- Work on your stance and gestures for a good performance.

- Always make your presentation from notes.

- Set the scene, pass out handouts, and grab the audience at once.

- With OHTs make them large, use colours, and leave them up.

- Props are essential: things often work better than pictures but data may need graphs to be understood.

- Pay attention to detail and stay in character.

- Decide how you will cope if you drop something.

- Emphasise the strong points of your product, *etc* and do not 'knock' the opposition.

- Always use positive language.

- When handling questions ignore the staff member, get eye contact with the questioner and use humour and props if you can.

11
Finishing Your First Year

NOTICING HOW YOU HAVE CHANGED

Towards the end of your first year it is a good idea to take stock and consider how you have changed since coming to university. It will boost your confidence, help with your motivation to study, and show you where you could make improvements in your second year.

Assessing the experience

Set aside an evening on your own to think and make a list of:

- what you have learned academically in broad terms
- the skills you have begun to develop
- the new experiences you have had
- the new places you have been
- the new friends you have made
- the problems you have encountered and how you've coped
- the areas where you can improve, *eg* the split between study and work.

Study the list, pat yourself on the back for the good parts and think about how you could improve. Then make a second list. On this write down what you will do better next year – this is your **second year resolution** list. Put the list in a safe place and dig it out when you come back.

PREPARING FOR YOUR SECOND YEAR

Your first year notes

It might seem tempting to throw out some of your first-year notes that you think you will never need again – do not do this! You can never be sure what you will need and you might need all of them.

Housing

If you have been lucky enough to get into university accommodation, you might have to move out at the end of the term. If you are even luckier and can stay a second year, you normally will not have to pay for the period you are away. You might however, have to pack up your stuff and store it in a trunk or suitcase somewhere in the building.

Sorting out next year's accommodation
Assuming you have to move out, early in the term consider your friends and decide who you think you could share with. You need to sort out how many bedrooms you need, the area you want to be in (a list of priorities might help), and the maximum you can afford to pay. Check the adverts in the local paper so that you get some idea of what you can expect to have to pay and/or talk to an estate agent in the area you would like to live. One of you could get back early and find a place, unless everybody wants to be involved in the decision.

Avoiding paying a retainer
If you have been in private accommodation, it is usually best to give it up rather than pay for the months when you will not be using it. It is unusual for a landlord to keep it for you without a retainer. If you give it up, next year you might have to pay a bit more elsewhere, but the difference in rent will probably be less than a retainer would be. You will also have more idea of what to look for, based on your experiences.

Checking out the second-year courses
You will probably have to make a decision about which subjects or courses you will study next year, especially if doing one of the newer modular degrees. This choice should not be rushed. It is a good idea to get advice, from your tutor, from any staff member you know, and from people in the second or third year. Your university calendar may have a list of the courses on offer but at best there will be bald descriptions with no indication of how good each course is. Your student union might have organised student evaluations of courses. These are often fascinatingly scurrilous, and will give you a much better idea of how interesting and well taught the courses are. If they say a course is **popular**, **interesting**, or **fun** this is attractive; but remember that **challenging, stimulating**, or **difficult but valuable** may offer better long-term prospects.

Choosing your subjects
When choosing what subjects to undertake, your main decision is between what interests you and what you think would appeal to an employer when you look for a job. Except for jobs requiring specific skills, like vets or accountants, most employers prefer to choose quality

students who can be trained to their particular needs. You can get a good job more easily if you have an upper second or first class degree, which indicates diligence and intelligence, than with a bare pass in subjects that relate to a particular industry.

Most people tend to score best at things that they enjoy, so you are usually better off choosing courses and subjects that interest you, rather than picking what you think an employer might want but that you will hate to study.

Thinking about job skills

Remember you need to develop job skills, like good communication, problem-solving ability, cooperative team working, organising tasks in priority order, and managing your time properly. If you took part in a team project or role-playing session in your first year you have made a good beginning and should try to do more if you can. You get better with practice. You might check to see if your university offers courses that directly teach such skills.

When you come to apply for jobs, these skills should be displayed in a prominent place on your CV. They not only impress, they also provide a good talking point at interviews and it gives you something valuable to say when asked those awful mind-numbing questions like 'What benefits do you think you got from going to university?', 'What are your strengths?' or 'Is there anything you would like to tell us?'

Looking ahead to the third year

You might also have a quick look in the university handbook for third-year courses to see if there any prerequisites set for subjects you might be interested in doing later. Sometimes you have to choose carefully in the second year to avoid being barred from something in the third.

Getting your book list

Once you have settled what you want to do next year, see if you can get a book list from the lecturer or the office. If you have the time, you could look at the set textbook during the vacation. If you decide early enough, you could ask your local library at home to order the book – your parents can do this for you. It is best not to buy a second-year textbook in your first year in case you change your mind and do a different subject. You can't trust the staff not to change the textbook in the interim either.

Studying in your second year

A trap to avoid as you prepare for your second year is the temptation to slacken off. It is a dangerous time when you feel completely at home at university but the end is still well out of sight (unlike for third-year students), so it is easy to revel in the apparent freedom, overindulge in socialising, and suffer reduced marks. This is a particular danger for those moving out of university accommodation into sharing a house with others.

ANTICIPATING GOING HOME

Assuming you have been to university in a new city, you will notice a difference when you go home.

The town and old friends may seem different

The town you remember fondly may seem small and perhaps even a bit boring after a time. You might wonder what you saw in some of the friends you left behind; they may seem parochial, small minded, and not as interesting as some of your new friends.

Seeing the change in your parents

Your parents might seem older than you remember when you haven't seen them for a while. They may perhaps be unable to understand what you are doing, how you spend your time, and why you are interested in all these crazy new things. Be prepared for questions about what you do at university but do not be surprised if your parents quickly lose interest when you try to explain.

What you are seeing is really a reflection of the changes in yourself. You are growing up and the changes in you are beginning to show but it can all be a little unsettling to go through.

After you get home

First you will probably need to relax and take a break from studying. Later, if you can face it, it is a good idea to do some preparatory reading for next year. If you make a crude timetable of what you want to do, or write down the names of a book or two you intend to read, it might strengthen your resolution. It is tempting to spend the whole vacation enjoying yourself, but if you can put aside say two or three weeks to do some preparation work, you will feel the benefit next year. If you are working on a vacation job for the entire period, too bad! Try to get at least a couple of weeks off to rest and recharge your batteries before you go back to university.

Remember! **Next year will be even better** – you are an old hand now, and will shortly have a new intake of freshers to critically examine as a new and perhaps slightly inferior species. You also have two more years of a great way to live. **Enjoy it!**

CASE STUDIES

Alan decides how he can improve

Alan thinks about what he has done and determines to tackle his weak spots which are mainly in essay writing. He has done well in team work and role-playing which pulls his overall mark up to a respectable B +. He is steadily improving and is looking forward to his second year. He chooses next year's courses with an eye on the banking job he wants. This, however, includes one course which he feels sounds boring. He may be storing up trouble here as gaining a good mark in this subject will be hard for him. He has no housing problem to consider and his wife is still supportive.

Jane's careful choice of course will pay off

Jane carefully goes over the year and correctly decides that boosting her self-confidence is the main area where she can improve. She decides she will find a study group and also join the drama society to help her gain self-assurance. She looked into next year's courses and consulted the students' union guide. She is generally selecting courses that sound interesting and challenging and has deliberately picked on one with a major oral presentation component so that she can carry on improving her presentation skills. She is still living with her parents but is starting to think that it might be good to share a house in her third year.

Bob takes little care choosing his courses

Bob did not even think of summing up his year and just wants to get home. He is relieved to have scraped through to the second year. Next year he intends to share a house with three other students and thinks it will be fun. He is unaware though, that he might have to struggle even more against the temptation to go out socialising and drinking. He chooses his second-year courses quickly and only bothers to do this because he is forced to fill in a form. He chooses those whose titles sounded easy, and one that someone told him was fun, but he didn't check this with anyone else. As a result his overall selection is a bit of a mishmash. He is also in for a shock next year, because one of the subjects he has chosen needs a lot of maths and he doesn't know this. He will have to drop it and find something else that he can do. This is unlikely to fit well with his other selections.

DISCUSSION POINTS

1. What subjects have you enjoyed most during the year? Which the least? Can you work out why that is? What does this suggest for

your choice of subjects in the second year?

2. What skills have you developed over the year? Which area do you think is most in need of improvement?

3. If you have to move into new accommodation next year, what exactly will you be looking for? Who will you share with? In which area would you prefer to live?

SUMMARY

- Make a list of what you have achieved and another list of what you can do to improve.

- If renting privately it is often best to give up your accommodation during the vacation.

- If you need to share accommodation, choose the people carefully.

- Consider the area you would like to live in and the maximum rent you can pay.

- Check out the second-year courses and try to choose what interests you.

- Courses involving skills of communication, problem-solving, and team work can help you get a job.

- Ask in the student union if they have done course appraisals.

- Try to get a book list of your chosen courses and do some reading for next year.

- Beware of the danger of slackening off in the second year.

- Be prepared to notice some differences when you go home.

Glossary

Assistant lecturer. A relatively low-level teaching staff member. In some universities this is the lowest level of staff.

CD-Rom. A computer disk, read-only, which contains information. Many libraries store valuable information on them.

Chancellor. An honorary position without real power, often occupied by someone famous.

Course code. The number that indicates a particular course. The university computer tends to need this.

Course. Usually means the entire range of subjects you are studying.

Degree. The valuable piece of paper you are working to earn. The common ones are BA (Bachelor of Arts), and BSc (Bachelor of Science). Increasingly other letters are being added to indicate the nature of the degree, *eg* BALaw or BAdmin. Higher degrees are the MA (Master of Arts) and above that the PhD (Doctor of Philosophy). The latter can be earned in any discipline, not just philosophy.

Discipline. Tends to refer to a precise study area, like mathematics, biology or economics. Some newer study areas may contain bits of different disciplines rather than be one, *eg* media studies.

Dissertation. An extended essay which explores a chosen subject in depth and which is normally only required for an MA or PhD degree.

Dr. Anyone who has earned a PhD degree.

Faculty staff. The academics who teach and undertake research.

Fresher week. The week before teaching begins in the first term, when the new students arrive.

Freshers. New students – used to be known as 'freshmen'.

General staff. The non-academics who manage and administer the university. Sometimes called administrative staff.

Graduate. As a noun, anyone who has passed an ordinary degree. As a verb, to finish an entire university course satisfactorily and be awarded your degree.

Honours. A higher level degree than an ordinary pass degree. Many three-year courses are deemed to be honours degrees, but some require a special fourth year. They are divided into first class (first), upper second class (two-one), lower second class (two-two) and third (pass).

Internet. The mass of computers in the world which can be accessed electronically. Useful information can be obtained but it is often hidden amongst a lot of rubbish.

Junior Common Room (JCR). The tea and coffee room for undergraduates.

Lecture. Where a staff member instructs you by reading or speaking aloud. It is essentially a one-way process, but some universities or lecturers allow or even encourage questions.

Lecturer. A middle-level member of the academic staff.

Multiple choice questions. Increasingly used in examinations, you select from a range of answer choices (A, B, C, D, *etc*) and my have to enter your choice on a special computer sheet.

Open book examination. An exam where you are allowed to bring in books to help you answer the questions.

Postgraduate. Anyone who has obtained a first degree (not 'first-class' degree) and is continuing to study to gain a higher degree.

Professor. The highest ranking of academic staff. In the United States it often means anyone teaching at a university.

Reader. A staff member one down from a Professor. At one time they did no teaching and concentrated on research, but that has usually changed these days.

Refectory. The place where you can buy lunch and maybe other snacks and meals. Many universities call it by a different name.

Registrar. The top person on the administrative side, who manages the university and is subordinate to the Vice-Chancellor.

Semester. There are two teaching semesters a year, so a semester is half the year. Compare with 'term'.

Seminar. A learning session in which a prepared paper is read out to the group and then opened up to questions and discussion.

Senior Common Room (SCR). Where the academics and very high level general staff drink tea and coffee.

Senior lecturer. A middle- to high-level staff member.

Subject. Refers to a study area. In some universities it is a limited area and you may study several subjects at the same time. In other universities it may refer to your entire course.

Teaching assistant. Usually the lowest level of staff. Not all universities have them.

Term. The year is divided into three teaching periods, known as terms. They may be numbered (first, second and third term) or in some old universities they may have a name (Lent, Easter, Michaelmas or Hilary, Trinity and Michaelmas).

Term (or semester) paper. A paper you prepare and write over a period of time and hand in for assessment. It is expected to be longer and better than, for instance, a weekly paper.

Tutorial. In some universities it means a few (maybe 2–5) students meeting with a staff member to listen to and discuss a tutorial paper. In other universities there may be as many as 30 students present.

Tutorial paper. A paper prepared and delivered by a student to a staff member and perhaps several other students. You write it out fully and read it aloud.

Vice-Chancellor. The most important person in the university, who runs it.

Workshop. A learning session where you go and *do* something as opposed to listen to a prepared paper.

Further Reading

Critical Thinking for Students: How to use your recommended texts on a university or college course, Roy van den Brink-Budgen (How To Books, 1996).

Going to University, Dennis Farrington (How To Books, 1996).

Good Study Guide, The, Andrew Northedge (Open University, 1990).

Handbook of Study Skills, The, Neil Burdess (Prentice Hall, 1991).

How to Pass Exams Without Anxiety, David Acres (How To Books, 4th ed 1995).

How to Study, Harry Maddox (Pan, 1988).

How to Study & Learn, Peter Marshall (How To Books, 1995).

How to Write an Assignment, Pauline Smith (How To Books, 2nd ed 1995).

How to Write Your Dissertation, Ray Swetnam (How To Books, 1995).

Study!, Robert Barras (Chapman & Hall, 1984).

Study Skills, Kate Williams (Macmillan Professional Masters, 1989).

Studying for a Degree, Stephen Wade (How To Books, 1996).

Writing an Essay, Brendan Hennessy (How To Books, 3rd ed 1996).

Index

How To Books provide practical help on a large range of topics. They are available through all good bookshops or can be ordered direct from the distributors. Just tick the titles you want and complete the form on the following page.

___ Apply to an Industrial Tribunal (£7.99)
___ Applying for a Job (£7.99)
___ Applying for a United States Visa (£15.99)
___ Be a Freelance Journalist (£8.99)
___ Be a Freelance Secretary (£8.99)
___ Be a Local Councillor (£8.99)
___ Be an Effective School Governor (£9.99)
___ Become a Freelance Sales Agent (£9.99)
___ Become an Au Pair (£8.99)
___ Buy & Run a Shop (£8.99)
___ Buy & Run a Small Hotel (£8.99)
___ Cash from your Computer (£9.99)
___ Career Planning for Women (£8.99)
___ Choosing a Nursing Home (£8.99)
___ Claim State Benefits (£9.99)
___ Communicate at Work (£7.99)
___ Conduct Staff Appraisals (£7.99)
___ Conducting Effective Interviews (£8.99)
___ Copyright & Law for Writers (£8.99)
___ Counsel People at Work (£7.99)
___ Creating a Twist in the Tale (£8.99)
___ Creative Writing (£9.99)
___ Critical Thinking for Students (£8.99)
___ Do Voluntary Work Abroad (£8.99)
___ Do Your Own Advertising (£8.99)
___ Do Your Own PR (£8.99)
___ Doing Business Abroad (£9.99)
___ Emigrate (£9.99)
___ Employ & Manage Staff (£8.99)
___ Find Temporary Work Abroad (£8.99)
___ Finding a Job in Canada (£9.99)
___ Finding a Job in Computers (£8.99)
___ Finding a Job in New Zealand (£9.99)
___ Finding a Job with a Future (£8.99)
___ Finding Work Overseas (£9.99)
___ Freelance DJ-ing (£8.99)
___ Get a Job Abroad (£10.99)
___ Get a Job in America (£9.99)
___ Get a Job in Australia (£9.99)
___ Get a Job in Europe (£9.99)
___ Get a Job in France (£9.99)
___ Get a Job in Germany (£9.99)
___ Get a Job in Hotels and Catering (£8.99)
___ Get a Job in Travel & Tourism (£8.99)
___ Get into Films & TV (£8.99)
___ Get into Radio (£8.99)
___ Get That Job (£6.99)
___ Getting your First Job (£8.99)
___ Going to University (£8.99)
___ Helping your Child to Read (£8.99)
___ Investing in People (£8.99)
___ Invest in Stocks & Shares (£8.99)

___ Keep Business Accounts (£7.99)
___ Know Your Rights at Work (£8.99)
___ Know Your Rights: Teachers (£6.99)
___ Live & Work in America (£9.99)
___ Live & Work in Australia (£12.99)
___ Live & Work in Germany (£9.99)
___ Live & Work in Greece (£9.99)
___ Live & Work in Italy (£8.99)
___ Live & Work in New Zealand (£9.99)
___ Live & Work in Portugal (£9.99)
___ Live & Work in Spain (£7.99)
___ Live & Work in the Gulf (£9.99)
___ Living & Working in Britain (£8.99)
___ Living & Working in China (£9.99)
___ Living & Working in Hong Kong (£10.99)
___ Living & Working in Israel (£10.99)
___ Living & Working in Japan (£8.99)
___ Living & Working in Saudi Arabia (£12.99)
___ Living & Working in the Netherlands (£9.99)
___ Lose Weight & Keep Fit (£6.99)
___ Make a Wedding Speech (£7.99)
___ Making a Complaint (£8.99)
___ Manage a Sales Team (£8.99)
___ Manage an Office (£8.99)
___ Manage Computers at Work (£8.99)
___ Manage People at Work (£8.99)
___ Manage Your Career (£8.99)
___ Managing Budgets & Cash Flows (£9.99)
___ Managing Meetings (£8.99)
___ Managing Your Personal Finances (£8.99)
___ Market Yourself (£8.99)
___ Master Book-Keeping (£8.99)
___ Mastering Business English (£8.99)
___ Master GCSE Accounts (£8.99)
___ Master Languages (£8.99)
___ Master Public Speaking (£8.99)
___ Obtaining Visas & Work Permits (£9.99)
___ Organising Effective Training (£9.99)
___ Pass Exams Without Anxiety (£7.99)
___ Pass That Interview (£6.99)
___ Plan a Wedding (£7.99)
___ Prepare a Business Plan (£8.99)
___ Publish a Book (£9.99)
___ Publish a Newsletter (£9.99)
___ Raise Funds & Sponsorship (£7.99)
___ Rent & Buy Property in France (£9.99)
___ Rent & Buy Property in Italy (£9.99)
___ Retire Abroad (£8.99)
___ Return to Work (£7.99)
___ Run a Local Campaign (£6.99)
___ Run a Voluntary Group (£8.99)
___ Sell Your Business (£9.99)

How To Books

___ Selling into Japan (£14.99)
___ Setting up Home in Florida (£9.99)
___ Spend a Year Abroad (£8.99)
___ Start a Business from Home (£7.99)
___ Start a New Career (£6.99)
___ Starting to Manage (£8.99)
___ Starting to Write (£8.99)
___ Start Word Processing (£8.99)
___ Start Your Own Business (£8.99)
___ Study Abroad (£8.99)
___ Study & Learn (£7.99)
___ Study & Live in Britain (£7.99)
___ Studying at University (£8.99)
___ Studying for a Degree (£8.99)
___ Successful Grandparenting (£8.99)
___ Successful Mail Order Marketing (£9.99)
___ Successful Single Parenting (£8.99)
___ Survive at College (£4.99)
___ Survive Divorce (£8.99)
___ Surviving Redundancy (£8.99)
___ Take Care of Your Heart (£5.99)
___ Taking in Students (£8.99)
___ Taking on Staff (£8.99)
___ Taking Your A-Levels (£8.99)
___ Teach Abroad (£8.99)
___ Teach Adults (£8.99)
___ Teaching Someone to Drive (£8.99)
___ Travel Round the World (£8.99)
___ Use a Library (£6.99)

___ Use the Internet (£9.99)
___ Winning Consumer Competitions (£8.99)
___ Winning Presentations (£8.99)
___ Work from Home (£8.99)
___ Work in an Office (£7.99)
___ Work in Retail (£8.99)
___ Work with Dogs (£8.99)
___ Working Abroad (£14.99)
___ Working as a Holiday Rep (£9.99)
___ Working in Japan (£10.99)
___ Working in Photography (£8.99)
___ Working in the Gulf (£10.99)
___ Working on Contract Worldwide (£9.99)
___ Working on Cruise Ships (£9.99)
___ Write a CV that Works (£7.99)
___ Write a Press Release (£9.99)
___ Write a Report (£8.99)
___ Write an Assignment (£8.99)
___ Write an Essay (£7.99)
___ Write & Sell Computer Software (£9.99)
___ Write Business Letters (£8.99)
___ Write for Publication (£8.99)
___ Write for Television (£8.99)
___ Write Your Dissertation (£8.99)
___ Writing a Non Fiction Book (£8.99)
___ Writing & Selling a Novel (£8.99)
___ Writing & Selling Short Stories (£8.99)
___ Writing Reviews (£8.99)
___ Your Own Business in Europe (£12.99)

To: Plymbridge Distributors Ltd, Plymbridge House, Estover Road, Plymouth PL6 7PZ.
Customer Services Tel: (01752) 202301. Fax: (01752) 202331.

Please send me copies of the titles I have indicated. Please add postage & packing (UK £1, Europe including Eire, £2, World £3 airmail).

☐ I enclose cheque/PO payable to Plymbridge Distributors Ltd for £ [   ]

☐ Please charge to my ☐ MasterCard, ☐ Visa, ☐ AMEX card.

Account No. [   ]

Card Expiry Date [   ] 19 [   ]   ☎ Credit Card orders may be faxed or phoned.

Customer Name (CAPITALS) ....

Address ....

.... Postcode ....

Telephone .... Signature ....

Every effort will be made to despatch your copy as soon as possible but to avoid possible disappointment please allow up to 21 days for despatch time (42 days if overseas). Prices and availability are subject to change without notice.

[Code BPA]